Simple Country Pleasures

A collection of fresh recipes, garden gifts & easy how-to's sprinkled with sweet country memories

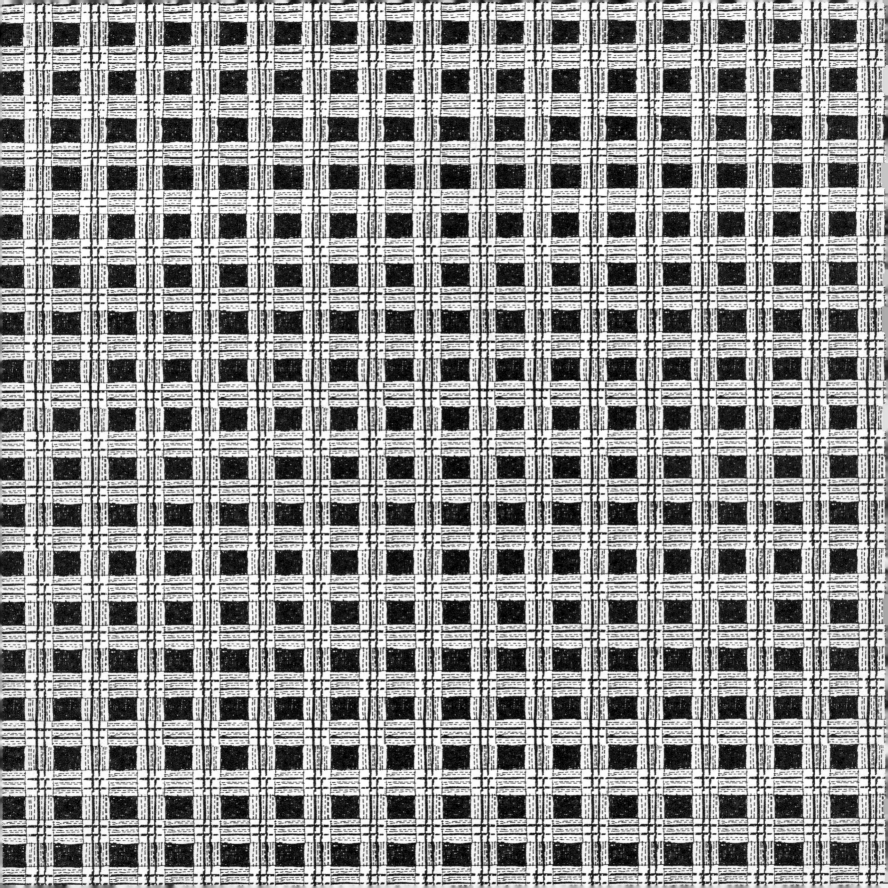

THE BEST OF
Gooseberry Patch CO. ™

Simple Country Pleasures

A collection of fresh recipes, garden gifts & easy how·to's sprinkled with sweet country memories

FRIEDMAN/FAIRFAX
PUBLISHERS

A GOOSEBERRY PATCH AND FRIEDMAN/FAIRFAX BOOK

© 1998 by Michael Friedman Publishing Group, Inc.

Library of Congress Cataloging-in-Publication Data
available upon request.

ISBN 1-56799-632-9

Editor: Francine Hornberger
Art Director: Jeff Batzli
Design: Elan Studio
Production Director: Karen Matsu Greenberg
Cover Art: Gooseberry Patch

Printed and bound in Great Britain by
Butler & Tanner Ltd, Frome and London

1 3 5 7 9 10 8 6 4 2

For bulk purchases and special sales, please contact:
Friedman/Fairfax Publishers
Attention: Sales Department
15 West 26th Street
New York, New York 10010
212/685-6610   FAX 212/685-1307

Visit our website:
http://www.metrobooks.com

Contents

★ ★ ★ ★ ★ ★ ★ ★ ★ ★ ★ ★ ★ ★ ★ ★ ★ ★ ★

Acknowledgments

★ ★ ★ ★ ★ ★ ★ ★ ★ ★ ★ ★ ★ ★ ★ ★ ★ ★

Our thanks to each one of you who shared your family traditions, recipes, and favorite holiday tips and ideas…you made this book possible. We continue to be overwhelmed by your response and generosity in welcoming us into your lives and sharing with us your warmest and most treasured Spring and Summertime memories, tips, and recipes. To all of you who have shared your thoughts and suggestions with **Gooseberry Patch** over the years, and for those whose names do not appear here, our heartfelt thanks for your contributions.

Betty Asberry
Peg Ackerman
Cora Baker
Jo Baker
Karyl Bannister
Jennifer Bieniek
Judy Borecky
Jennifer Broski
Cathy Brown
Barbara Burnham
Maggie Cambron
Julie Carwille

Barbara Bargdill
Edith Beck
Delores Berg
Sheri Berger
Sandy Bessingpas

Sue Carbaugh
Myrtle Christ
Donna Crawford
Charlotte Crockett
Sandra Curtis
Deb Damari-Tull
Mary Dechamplain
Linda Desmond
Diane Donato
Kristen Eddy
Jeaninne English
Kathy Epperly
Janice Ertola
Cheryl Ewer
Debbie Felt
Christel Zuber Fishburn
Diann Fox
Marie Alana Gardner

Katherine Gaughan
Nancie Gensler
Peggy Gerch
Denise Green
Therese Gribbins
Tamara Gruber
Frances Guch
Jolie Halm
Gay Hanbi
Judy Hand
Candy Hannigan
Vicki Hockenberry

Laura Hodges
Heather Hood
Starlette Howard
Jacqueline Lash-Idler
Jan Jacobson
Carol Jones
Marsha Jones
Shirll Kosmal
Dawn Lee
Linda Lee
Glenda Lewis
Barbara Loe
Theresa Manley
Barbara Rose
    McCaffrey
Barb McFaden
Shelley McHugh
Diane Michaels
Janet Mitrovich
Donna Moran
Natalie
    Morrissette

Deborah Murray
Mary Murray
Susan Mroz
Glenda Nations
Loretta Nichols
MaryAnne Osesek
Wendy Lee Paffenroth
Crystal Parker
Debbie Parker
Deborah Peters
Phyllis Peters
Kathryn Pedrazzoli
Marion Pfeifer

Elizabeth Phillips
Cheryl Porada
Margaret Riley
Ronda Rivers-Stone
Arlene Roberts
Glenna Ryder
Amy Schueddig
Judy Sculze
Lisa Sett
Toni Shawl
Carol Sheets
Jan Sofranko
Carol Steels

Doris Stegner
Jean Stokes
Rebecca Suiter
Elizabeth Timmins
Michelle Urdahl
Karen Wald
Amy Walker
Deb Weiser
Marlene Wetzel-
    Dellagatta
Mary Wighall
Mel Wolk
Margaret Zellhofer

Introduction

★ ★ ★ ★ ★ ★ ★ ★ ★ ★ ★ ★ ★ ★ ★ ★ ★ ★ ★

Dear Friends,

Like a breath of fresh, clean country air, **Simple Country Pleasures** captures the joys of everyday living! Each whimsical chapter invites you to savor the little things…the sparkle of stars scattered across a midnight sky, the cheerful chirping of crickets, the joyful songs of birds and the sweet smell of a fresh morning breeze.

Take a carefree trip to the country with **Gooseberry Patch**…explore the "Potting Shed," where tender gifts that grow are created. Join us for "Traditions & Memories," sure to warm your heart. Relieve tensions and soothe stress with remedies and tips found in the "Herbal Pantry." Expressions of the heart mean the most when they're

"Handmade with Love," and we'll show you just how. And enjoy the rich aroma wafting from our "Country Kitchen," filled with inspiring recipes so easy, you'll have plenty of time to savor the results!

We've gathered our best ideas from friends across the country to bring you this very special book. Stop and spend some time with **Gooseberry Patch**...enjoy the country pleasures each day brings...and all the simple gifts along the way!

Wishing you simple joys,
        Vickie & JoAnn

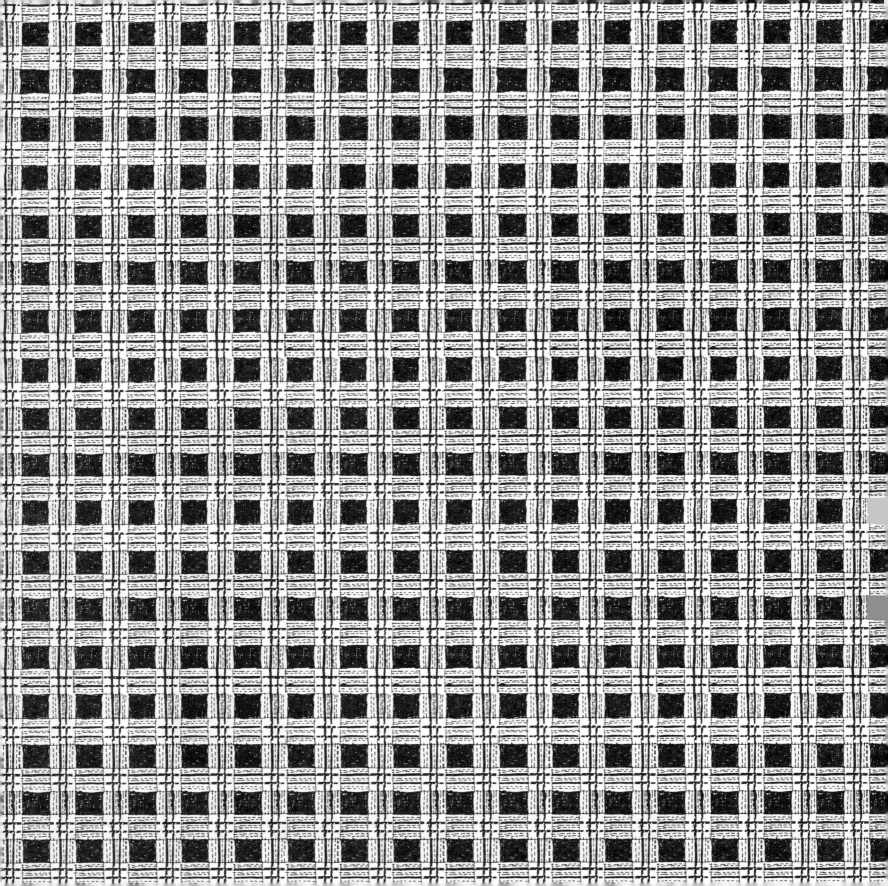

chapter one Traditions & Memories

Wonderful Memories

My grandfather could grow anything, even in the hot Texas sun. After my grandmother passed away, he made his home with us for ten years, until he joined her. All that time, he still planted a huge garden, tended fruit trees, and took care of all the flower beds. Of course, the plants that grew for him did not flourish for us after he was gone, for he truly had a "green thumb" and a closeness to the earth. I can still see him picking fresh cherry tomatoes, wiping them off, and popping them into his mouth. He grew flower beds full of what he called "pinks." They had a delicious fragrance and were so pretty. I can still see the rows and rows of colorful zinnias.

I have numerous gardening memories of my grandmother, who lived very frugally in a small mobile home much of her life, and who shared great wisdom in her love for God, family, and the things of the earth. There were always flowers in bloom (it seemed) at Grandma's doorstep, and she never failed to point out their beauty with exclamations like, "Isn't that the most glorious shade of blue you've ever seen?!" She had a certain "snap" that made life seem simple and pure. And I remember the great sunflowers that would tower over me, almost scary to a small child as they waved in the breeze. Yet it was those same sunflowers, out of which I picked the seeds, that taught me to care for God's creatures. I took great delight in throwing the seeds on the patio, running inside, and watching the birds feast. For me, the lessons of the garden from my grandmother produce growth far beyond what comes out of the soil.

Many years ago, before I had children, I worked in an office that looked out onto a vacant lot. Summer was always hard because I wanted to be outside working in the flowers, not inside at a desk. One year, I planted a single sunflower in that vacant lot and talked the maintenance people into mowing around it. All summer, from my desk inside, I watched that sunflower grow. I watched it bloom and the birds pull out the seeds for food in the fall. I finally watched it wither up and die with the first frost. That year, I did not miss summer at all.

★ ★ ★ ★ ★ ★ ★ ★ ★ ★ ★

The fragrance of certain flowers evokes memories of important occasions in my past. Geraniums bring back Mother's Day in Sunday school, lilacs our eighth-grade graduation, nasturtiums Grandmother's home.

Offer a touch of "welcome home" to your family or guests when they come to visit by adding some personal touches. For example, wreaths tied with cheery bows; baskets full of flowers or potted plants; a comfy rocker to pass the time resting in; or a set of wicker furniture with fat cushions you can sink down into. Around the porch, place benches, Welcome signs, and wind chimes to make magic in the air.

Summer Shade

It could have been just yesterday
The way memories are remade
That I claimed the canvas hammock
Hanging in the summer's shade.

In Grandma's wide backyard
With fruit ripening on the trees
I was young but had my dreams
And could do just as I pleased.

On days with clouds I'd see images
Or gaze dreamily at the blue
Pushing myself back and forth
I could linger the whole day through.

And might have done just that
If it weren't for fresh lemonade
Topped with just a sprig of mint
Served at a table in the shade.

It could have been just yesterday
But many a year has gone
But when I think of summer...
These memories linger on.

My advice to you is not to inquire why...
but just enjoy your ice cream
while it's on your plate.
That's my philosophy.
—Thornton Wilder

During the summer, my sisters and I would pick clover, tie the flowers together to make a chain, and then wear them as bracelets and necklaces. We also picked yellow buttercup flowers and held them to each other's neck. If yellow appeared on our necks from the reflection, it meant that we liked butter! How simple and refreshing those days were...little girls romping and playing in the grass.

★ ★ ★ ★ ★ ★ ★ ★ ★ ★ ★ ★ ★ ★ ★ ★

These were the rules of my grandmother's garden:
• Organize gardening supplies
• Talk to husband
• Reorganize gardening supplies
• Talk to husband
• Forget whole gardening thing
• Talk to self!
She kept these rules on a card with her salad recipes. She was a very jolly and humorous lady!

One of my favorite memories is my mother purchasing bushels of black-eyed peas, corn, green beans. We spent several summer afternoons shelling, peeling, or whatever was necessary to get these ready to freeze or can. At about 3:00 we would take a break for some cold watermelon. Mother would make preserves from the peaches of our three peach trees, and that taste just can't be found anymore. In early spring, a favorite family Sunday dinner was a garden smorgasbord...fresh green beans with potatoes, green onions, leaf lettuce salad, corn-on-the-cob, boiled squash sweetened with sugar, fried okra, sliced tomatoes, and cornbread. Such simple pleasures are life's best.

Mary, Mary, quite contrary,
How does your garden grow?
With silver bells, and cockleshells,
And pretty maids all in a row.

Dear Grandma
I am coming
to see you
this Summer
and Grandpa
too. I Love
you. xoxoxo
Love
Emily
P.S. I made pictures

me ➤
Grandma

As a child of the Depression, I made my very own toys and fun. My younger sister and cousins would join me. From the time school let out we would play outdoors, except for meals. In the spring the woods were ablaze with white dogwood. We figured out all by ourselves where to hide (usually a tree arbor, thicket, or bush). Scouring the meadows and woods daily, we would spend hours searching for wildflower plants...no one ever showed us where to look, or told us their names; it was instinct. We would stain pussy willows with colored chalk, and set Queen Anne's lace in water colored with food coloring (or mother's wash-day bluing), resulting in beautifully colored flowers. Skunk cabbage, violets, pussy willows, and countless other flowers grew in our glorious meadow, where we made hollyhock dolls and saw faces in the pansies. When we tore apart the bleeding hearts we imagined we could see two rabbits or two earrings. Swinging from wild grapevines we shrieked wildly, imitating Tarzan of the Apes. We chewed on sweet grasses and sipped drops of honey liquid from the honeysuckle. Every blackberry, elderberry, strawberry, gooseberry, and blueberry patch was known to us, and we kept each a well-guarded secret. We also knew where to find black cherries, beech, hickories, and the wild plum thickets. The sweet-scented crab apple blooms made wonderful wreaths, strung on a string between two sticks implanted in the ground. We played house and store, and begged posters of movie queens from the merchants. Picnics were often held on large boulders where my mother played as a girl. My aunt would treat us to cold watermelon, chilled in the well. She had a huge grape arbor over a structure of sorts. We would sit at a table there to eat meals and sip lemonade, when we were lucky enough to be asked.

> **Life isn't a matter of milestones but of moments.**
> —Rose Fitzgerald Kennedy

Our neighbor's wild pansy field was open for children to pick flowers. What a joy to seek the long stems, with a handful of tiny yellow blooms. I swiftly ran home to place them in a little glass bottle. I would deliver the vase of colorful pansies to an elderly neighbor. Each day, until the pansies stopped blooming, I walked amid the field and gathered lovely gifts for free. The repetition of this carefree task was a childhood delight creating lasting memories. I learned the beauty of sharing, and the joy of giving, which I carried into my adult life. May I pass it on to another generation.

For years, my boys, now 33 and 27, would bring me a bouquet of lilacs for Mother's Day. Every time I smell a lilac tree it brings back pleasant memories. They were the nicest flowers I ever received.

★ ★ ★ ★ ★ ★ ★ ★ ★ ★ ★ ★

When our sons were young, we started a tradition of casting their footprints, handprints, signatures, and the date in a cement stone or block every summer. The grandchildren have continued the tradition. Now, the stones are laid in a marvelous "sitting" patio in the garden. It is so great to record the growth and change in children through the years and it has made a wonderful conversation piece.

HOW TO PRESERVE CHILDREN

Take one large grassy field; ½ dozen children, all sizes; 3 small dogs; and one narrow strip of brook, pebbly if possible. Mix the children with the dogs and empty them into the field, stirring continually. Sprinkle with field flowers, pour brook gently over pebbles, cover all with a deep blue sky and bake in a hot sun. When the children are well-browned they may be removed. Will be found ready for setting away to cool in the bathtub.

Look up at those billowy, white clouds in the sky…what shapes do you see?

My grandpa and I were the best of friends. Grandma worked second shift, leaving the afternoons for just Grandpa and me. One summer afternoon, he sat in his lawn chair watching me as I played in my sandbox. When I would get so dirty he couldn't stand it, he would throw me in my swimming pool to clean me off a bit. Then, back into the sandbox I would go. This went on all afternoon. After hours of fun, it was time to settle down for the evening. That night when Grandma came in from work, she saw the two of us together, sound asleep and dirty from our head to our toes…only my eyelids were clean (because I never closed my eyes all day!). Every time my grandma tells this story she smiles and tears come to her eyes. My grandpa passed away over seven years ago, and remembering the "good old days" helps us remember what he meant to all of us.

RESERVED FOR GRANDMA

Good friends, good books,
and a sleepy conscience:
this is the ideal life.
—Mark Twain

When I was younger, staying at Grandma and Grandpa's was at the top of my list, especially in the summer. They had a garden so big I thought I might get lost in it, if I dared to enter alone. I always begged to pick all the vegetables. Grandma knew that peas were my favorite. She would chuckle when I came out of the garden with my pail, because she knew it would only be half full (the other half in my tummy). She would ask me, "How did they taste, dear?" Grandpa would bring a clean bowl from the house and we would shuck the peas on the front step. After we cleaned all the vegetables, Grandma would carry me into the house, sit me on the counter and wash off all the mud on my feet (gardening was much more fun when barefoot!). Grandpa is gone now, and Grandma doesn't garden as much as she used to, but the fond memories of staying at their house those long-ago summers live on.

Love is an irresistible desire
to be irresistibly desired.
—Robert Frost

The year my first child was born, I planted 100 red and yellow tulips under a large tree in our front yard. Every spring I set him in the mass of color and took his picture playing with the flowers. After many years, the tree roots crowded out the bulbs, and we moved from that house, but the pictures I took of him smiling in the tulips will last forever.

We loved picking rhubarb in the summer. After wearing a big rhubarb leaf as a sun hat, we would eat the stem. Our mouths puckered and our teeth danced but the fresh, tart taste was a shivery thrill!

Auntie Rae's Rhubarb

A man travels the world over in search of what he needs and returns home to find it.
—George Moore

The garden is a special place for me, especially being raised in an urban setting like San Francisco where garden space can be limited. The garden is where you come face to face with some of the wonders of the world...trails of ants carrying huge objects to and fro, butterflies landing on your hand for a snack of sugar water from a cotton ball, or the discovery of roly-polys (pill bugs) under a log. It's no wonder that the garden is also a favorite place of my daughter who chose to have her third birthday celebrated there. The activities and menu were themed around bugs and plants. For example, the sandwiches were sourdough rolls with their fixings arranged in the shape of a caterpillar on a platter. Olives and toothpicks were attached to the sides of each roll to form the "feet" of the caterpillar. The hit of the celebration was the unusual birthday cake which surprised everyone because it looked like a potted plant rather than the delicious pudding-and-cream surprise that it was. This dirt cake can be made the day before and takes less room in the refrigerator than a layered cake... great news for the busy hostess.

Inspiring Ideas

Each time a child (or grandchild) is born into your family, plant a tree in your garden. On each birthday, take a photograph of the child in front of "his" or "her" tree, and remember to date each picture. You can keep a special album of this yearly growth, or frame the photos and add to your collection as time goes by.

Great gifts for the gardener are birdhouses, tools, watering cans, garden books, journals, gift certificates to garden catalogs and stores, subscriptions to favorite gardening magazines, weather vanes, wind chimes, and signs.

Everyone needs a tree swing, the simplest and most wonderful of garden pleasures. Ours is hanging from an old pecan tree that overlooks my perennial garden. Kids love to swing and try to reach the very spot where the green earth ends and blue sky begins. For me, a swing is an absolute necessity. I hope I never outgrow swinging!

When shopping at garage sales, keep your eyes open for lightly loved teacups with saucers, sugar bowls and creamers, and beautiful old porcelain serving pieces, selling for very little. Small cracks and chips will only add character when the container is planted with a tiny blooming violet and given to a friend.

Go browsing at your garden store and plan, plan, plan! Before you buy, stop and give some thought to color combinations, height of plants, and planting so your garden will have color all summer long.

★ ★ ★ ★ ★ ★ ★ ★ ★ ★ ★ ★ ★ ★ ★ ★ ★ ★ ★

Buy sunflower seeds early. There are so many varieties and they will sell out fast.

Let your imagination run wild as you go from room to room looking for unusual containers for your house plants. Old hat boxes, wooden crates, wicker picnic baskets, the seat of an old chair, colorful old pottery bowls and crocks all make lovely containers. Have fun with your plants! Use a hat stand or peg rack to display an assortment of hanging plants.

★ ★ ★ ★ ★ ★ ★ ★ ★ ★ ★ ★ ★ ★ ★ ★ ★ ★ ★

When having an outdoor party for children, borrow your child's red wagon, fill it with ice, and put cold drinks and juice boxes in it. Be sure you clean the wagon first! You can also use a new garden hand spade to scoop ice into paper cups.

For sunburn or regular burns, use aloe vera plant or cider vinegar and water. When aloe leaves are broken, they emit a liquid that has remarkable healing qualities.

Remember, plants can be a great way to camouflage an eyesore. Try covering the side of your garage with lattice work or trellis netting. Plant hollyhocks, morning glories, and nasturtiums, or any vining plant. You'll love the results.

⋆ ⋆ ⋆ ⋆ ⋆ ⋆ ⋆ ⋆ ⋆ ⋆ ⋆ ⋆ ⋆ ⋆ ⋆ ⋆

A fun family game to play on a warm summer evening is to have a family squirt-gun fight. Fill 'em up and chase each other around the yard. Lots of laughs and great fun for all ages!

NIFTY IDEAS FOR PLANT CONTAINERS:

Old wagons…plant directly in the wagon or load up with lots of pots of colorful flowers.

Old or new barrel halves…plant a whole vegetable garden with extra loose, sandy soil for the carrots that can't possibly grow in your native clay.

How about a blueberry or raspberry bush in a barrel?

Or lots of flowers and a small birdbath in the middle of a barrel? Plant tallest plants in the middle, medium-size plants around the edge, and smaller, trailing plants around the sides. Drill holes in the sides and plant a strawberry gabble. Seal the inside and plant a waterlily for a small water garden.

Let the kids plant inside their old shoes for a "Grouch Garden," or in a small, plastic wading pool for a great veggie garden.

Large tin cans…the lovely enamel ones with pictures of tomatoes and olives are great.

Use buckets or watering cans… just poke in drainage holes.

The list is endless.
It's fun to use your imagination.

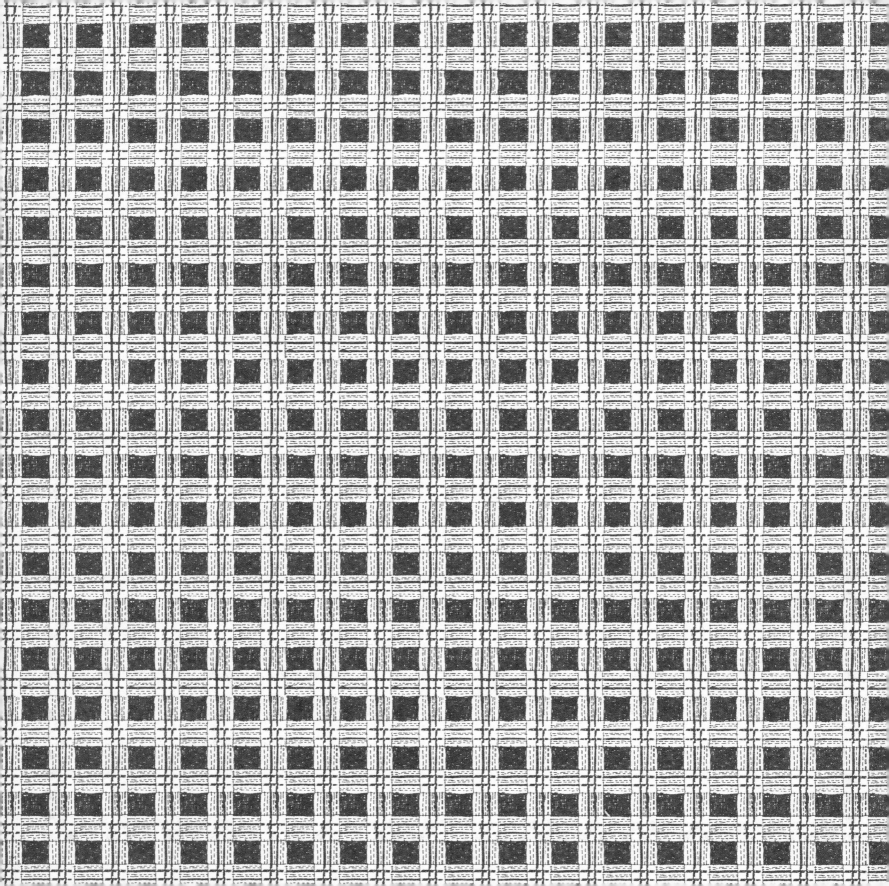

chapter two The Potting Shed

Tips from Our Readers

I like a lot of bird feeders in my garden but using birdseed made such a mess and sprouted weeds, so instead I use sunflower seeds. When the seeds fall as the birds eat, I have sunflowers that grow in the flower beds. Looks so pretty!

★ ★ ★ ★ ★ ★ ★ ★ ★ ★

When I cut fresh flowers from my garden, instead of those fancy, expensive flower preservers, I use a homemade one that contains three items found in every home. I fill my vase with water (8 oz.), add approximately ½ teaspoon of regular household bleach, and a teaspoon of sugar (sugar cubes work great). My flowers tend to last 2 to 3 weeks this way, sometimes even longer. Use double bleach if you keep your vase of flowers in direct sunlight.

> When cutting fresh flowers, place them immediately into a bucket of water you've carried with you. They'll stay fresh longer.

My husband and I made a winding path in our yard using old broken cement from our garage floor. We busted up big chunks of the floor, then dug out a path. It is in the shape of a long S. We laid the cement pieces, filled the dirt back in, and swept the path. Later we planted thyme and flowers in some of the gaps between the stones. It's gorgeous!

I'm always searching for old bird nests (especially the small, feathery-soft ones) and old birdhouses. I have them all over the house. Not only does this bring a little of the outdoors and nature inside, but you really marvel and appreciate the work and the wonder of nature when you see these close up. As a special Mother's Day gift this year, my two kids gave me a heart-shaped nest, nestled in between three branches. They had found it during the winter (when we find all of them) and wrapped it up. Any old birdhouse I see at any sale, I quickly grab! I have replicas of churches, houses, barns, and a chicken! They are amazing. I have them in my kitchen, dining and living rooms, in the garden, on my porch, and even atop my clothesline pole!
They are so homey and unique.

Store cuttings in a raw potato to keep them fresh during travel. Slice the potato in half lengthwise and place the cut ends inside the potato. Put a rubber band around the potato to hold it together.

What sweeter bouquet could a mother receive than a bunch of dandelions clutched in the hands of her small child?

I have found two ways to plant mint so that it does not take over my entire herb garden. For rather large areas of mint I use black plastic landscape edging. I follow the instructions for placing this in the ground, except that I dig deep enough to put it all the way into the ground. This way I can cover it with soil and mulch and it does not have to show at all. For containing mint in small spaces, I cut the bottom out of a thin plastic pot, place the mint in the pot, and bury the whole pot in the ground.

★ ★ ★ ★ ★ ★ ★ ★ ★ ★ ★ ★ ★

Not a slight change in the seasons or a holiday goes by that I do not decorate my fireplace mantel accordingly. It is the first thing you see as you walk in to my home and the results are beautiful! Spring arrives with my chalkware bunnies, old birdhouses, and a watering can. Summertime brings dried hydrangeas, bird nests, old fishing paraphernalia and baskets, with a few seashells added in. Let your imagination run wild! Of course there is always room for specific holiday items and treasures made by little hands that have been saved over the years.

To relieve sore muscles from bending while gardening, make hot compresses. Place a dampened finger towel in the microwave on high for 20 seconds; turn the towel over and microwave an additional 10–15 seconds.

Garden Tips

To keep flowers and herbs fresh longer, always cut stems with a knife instead of scissors; scissors crush the stems and they cannot absorb as much water.

✴ ✴ ✴ ✴ ✴ ✴ ✴ ✴ ✴ ✴ ✴ ✴ ✴ ✴ ✴

The most important thing about gardening is the soil. You can recognize poor soil if it's caked and forms clods, is difficult to cultivate, has lots of weeds, or your plants seem to be susceptible to diseases. Try adding humus (manure, peat, leaf mold). You'll get a better texture.

Before you work in your garden, push your fingernails into a bar of soap. After gardening, your nails will clean up quickly with a nail brush.

✴ ✴ ✴ ✴ ✴ ✴ ✴ ✴ ✴ ✴ ✴ ✴ ✴ ✴ ✴ ✴ ✴

Plant your herb and vegetable gardens as close to your back door as possible. Not only will your gardens be more convenient to use, but when you see them more often, you will be more likely to do the weeding, pruning, and harvesting needed to keep them looking good, and to notice any insect problems early.

POTTING MIX

Here's how to make your own potting mix for container gardening:

2 cubic ft. peat moss
40 oz. bag perlite
40 oz. bag vermiculite
1 handful 5-10-10 fertilizer
1 handful ground lime

Mix these ingredients well and make sure mixture is well soaked before adding plants. You will need to water more often when using this "soil," but the results will be well worth the effort.

When planting small bulbs, such as grape hyacinth, use an apple corer to dig the holes. It is the perfect size for small bulbs.

When pests strike, mix one tablespoon of dish-washing detergent with one cup of cooking oil. Then mix one to 1½ teaspoons of the detergent-oil mixture with each cup of water. The detergent causes the oil to emulsify in the water. It can be sprayed on plants every 10 days with a pump sprayer. For larger volume use 3 tablespoons of concentrated detergent-oil solution to one quart of water; or 12 tablespoons (approximately ⅓ cup) of detergent-oil solution to one gallon of water. Add one tablespoon baking soda per gallon to maintain alkaline pH. Besides aphids and white-flies, the mixture works against spider mites and beet army worms (don't they sound dreadful?). It has been used successfully on eggplant, carrots, lettuce, celery, water-melon, peppers, and cucumbers, but tends to burn the leaves of squash, cauliflower, and red cabbage.

Think about locating your children's wading pool where the draining water will automatically water your vegetables or flowers. You may not have to water your garden at all with strategic pool placement and lots of mulch!

An easy way to keep up with all of your garden work is to do a little bit each day. Spending just 15 minutes a day can take the place of a whole afternoon of gardening once a week.

Use spring-type clothespins to train vines and climbing plants.

Put a scented geranium in a pot by your backdoor. When you brush by it, it will release a delightful scent.

To control the slug and snail population growth in your vegetable garden, simply spread bran (available at feed stores) around the base of the plants. A natural way to protect your veggies!

* *

When planting a tree or shrub, remember this tip on fertilizing. Put an ounce of fertilizer in a plastic bag, punch holes in the bag, then bury it in a hole 6 to 12 inches from the shrub and 6 inches deep. It will keep fertilizing for several seasons.

* *

If you select a planting container that may possibly need to be moved, lighten the load with a simple trick. If the planter is large and filling it completely with soil would cause it to be too heavy, fill the container half full with used aluminum soda pop cans, or leftover Styrofoam packing "peanuts." The top half of the container should be filled with potting soil.

There are beneficial insects that you want to attract to your garden. They are natural enemies of some of the pests that gardeners are always trying to get rid of. Plants such as dill, spearmint, white clover, and lemon-scented marigold will attract the right kind of bugs!

* *

The worst enemies of successful seed storage are humidity and heat. Most varieties will keep until the next season. Buy your parsley, lettuce, and onions fresh each year. Ziplock freezer bags or sealed jars are ideal for storing. Keep your seeds in your coolest room or the refrigerator.

HOSTA

BLEEDING HEART

To grow a new rose bush, cut a stem with a full bloom rose on it. Stick the stem into the ground. Leave a few of the leaves at the top, with the bloom. Water the ground thoroughly and put a clear glass jar over it and anchor to the ground. Keep soil watered around jar every day until frost. Don't remove glass jar until next spring. You will then have a new rose bush growing. To give your plants an "extra" boost, add one teaspoon of Epsom salts and one teaspoon of fish emulsion plant fertilizer to your brand of plant fertilizer, then stand back and watch the results!

* * * * * * * * * * * * * * * * *

To plant tiny seeds such as lettuce and carrots, I start with a can (a soup can will work fine) half full of fine, dry soil. I then put in the seeds and shake the can to mix the seeds with the soil. Then, I slowly pour the seed-soil mix along the rows. The seeds won't blow away and they will be evenly spaced.

Try at least one new plant each year. It could be a flower, herb, or vegetable.

Use a bay leaf in your flour canister to keep the bugs out all year!

Ever have trouble figuring out what fertilizer to use? Those three numbers on the front of the bag refer to nitrogen, phosphorus, and potassium, and they are always in that order. Generally speaking, nitrogen is thought to improve leaf development, phosphorus is for flower and seed growth, and potassium promotes healthy root growth and allows the other two nutrients to work. So if your flowers aren't blooming very well, try a fertilizer with a high middle number.

* * * * * * * * * * * * * * * * * *

Plant bulbs about three times their diameter deep, measuring from the "shoulder" (where the bulb starts to flare out) of the bulb. If your soil is wet, dig down a couple of inches deeper and put about an inch of builder's sand (coarse, sharp sand available at sand and gravel companies) at the bottom of the hole. Add the recommended amount of bulb food and/or bone meal, cover with an inch of dirt to keep the fertilizer from damaging the bulb, then plant the bulb...pointed end up. If you're not sure which end of the bulb should be up, plant it on its side.

If you have problems with cats in your garden beds, sprinkle ground citrus peels and cayenne pepper on the soil.

★ ★ ★ ★ ★ ★ ★ ★ ★ ★ ★ ★ ★ ★ ★ ★ ★

If you want to start seeds indoors, set your flats on a table and hang lights on S hooks with light chains from the ceiling in a warm basement or other room. The lights must be no more than 3 to 6 inches from the top of the flat (or the plants, when they start growing), so be sure to make your light set-up adjustable. Plain old fluorescent shop lights work best for starting seeds, full spectrum or "grow lights" are just for growing blooming plants indoors, and are very expensive.

Whiteflies are tiny sucking insects that feed and lay eggs on the undersides of leaves. Hang a yellow cord coated with mineral oil in the infested area. Whiteflies are attracted to yellow, and will get caught in the oil.

★ ★ ★ ★ ★ ★ ★ ★ ★ ★ ★ ★ ★ ★ ★ ★ ★

To increase the growth and output of your tomato plants, buy plants that are about one foot tall or grow them to this height in a seed pot. When transplanting them in the garden, first dig a hole about the length of the plant, then cut all but the top cluster of leaves from the stem. Place the plant into the hole and bury it to within 2 inches of the top leaves. This will increase your root structure and therefore help each plant to produce more tomatoes.

> **Plant peppers between tomato plants and you won't have tomato worms or blight.**

When purchasing plants, resist the temptation to buy the larger ones in full bloom. These plants have already reached their peak. Instead pick the youngest plants, they will have a much longer flowering season. At least once a week, remove dead and faded blooms from your plants and they will continue to produce more blooms.

★ ☆ ★ ☆ ★ ☆ ★ ☆ ★ ☆ ★ ☆ ★ ☆ ★ ☆ ★ ☆ ★

Cut off the bottom of a large plastic trash can. Fill with garden and yard clippings, kitchen peels and leftovers; keep covered. After a period of time, empty from the bottom and work into the soil as fertilizer.

Spray your compost pile with a cola to speed the decaying process.

With increasing awareness of protecting the environment, many gardeners are turning to the benefits of composting. Most know the basics… no fats, grease, or animal products, just plant-type material; keep compost evenly moist (not drenched), aerated, and turn it frequently. Composting can be a lengthy process, but a simple step can speed up the process. Simply put proper composting material in blender or food processor and grind for a few seconds. Breaking the material into much smaller particles will greatly speed up the composting process. Only well-composted material should be used in the garden, because material that still needs to decompose will take energy out of the soil for the composting process, and thus rob plants of nutrients.

★ ★ ★ ★ ★ ★ ★ ★ ★ ★ ★ ★ ★ ★ ★ ★ ★

When trimming shrubs, lay a plastic tarp under the bushes to catch the clippings. Upon completion, just roll up the tarp and funnel the trimmings into the yard waste can. This procedure saves cleanup time and back bending pickup work. An added bonus is that the decorative bark doesn't get thrown away with the clippings.

What eats thousands of insects a year and is the best friend an organic gardener can have? A toad, of course! Are you lucky enough to have a pond in your garden? (No fish, they eat toad eggs). Or do you have an area near your garden that you don't mind leaving unmowed and natural? Perfect toad hiding places! You may already have a toad or two on nightly insect patrol. Toads have a voracious appetite for grasshoppers, cutworms, slugs, and flies (all the insects that drive gardeners crazy!). It is very important that ABSOLUTELY NO PESTICIDES are used in the garden, as they are easily absorbed through the toad's skin. There are many books available on amphibians and backyard ponds. It is well worth the effort to attract and keep these insect-eating machines.

When planting green pepper plants in your garden, drop two or three matches in the hole before you put the green pepper plant in. The sulfur in the matches makes the plants produce more peppers.

Keep a stone or file handy to maintain a relatively sharp blade on shovels, forks, and hoes.

Weeding after a rain is the best time; the roots are looser.

Companion planting, or planting certain plants near others, is effective in keeping pests away. When planted with tomatoes, mint repels tomato hornworm; with radish, flea beetles; and with cabbage, white cabbage butterflies. Horseradish keeps away potato bugs; garlic and nasturtiums will keep aphids at bay; and marigolds repel tomato hornworm, nematodes, and whiteflies.

A quick once-over with a stiff bristle brush or aluminum foil will remove caked-on soil from garden tools. You may wish to scrape the tool with a putty knife before brushing.

A 5-gallon bucket filled with oily sand is an excellent way to store shovels, pitchforks, hoes, and spades. Otherwise, coat them with a thin film of oil, using an old rag, before putting away.

When staking tomato plants or other vegetable plants, use strips of old nylon stockings or pantyhose to tie the plants to the stake. The nylons will stretch as the plant grows.

When planting seeds in the garden, use an empty spice shaker with holes in the top to sprinkle them. Mix fine seeds with unflavored powdered gelatin. It will release a little nitrogen as it breaks down, and the color of the gelatin powder will help you see where you are sowing the seeds as you go.

* * * * * * * * * * * * * * * * * * * *

Mold will grow on plants if they do not have time to dry out properly. Watering in the early morning will help discourage this problem.

A swarm of bees in May
Is worth a load of hay;
A swarm of bees in June
Is worth a silver spoon;
A swarm of bees in July
Is not worth a fly.
—Old English proverb

Use lunch-size snack cups from gelatins, and puddings for starting seeds. Punch small holes in base of each cup for drainage and line up cups in large flats from a garden center.

* * * * * * * * * * * * * * * * * * * *

Annually put a few drops of machine oil on the bolts and springs of tools before using.

* * * * * * * * * * * * * * * * * * * *

Flowers can be a natural pest control while making your garden more beautiful and pleasurable to work in. For example, daisies, black-eyed Susans, and yarrow attract beneficial insects to their pollen and nectar. Then these good insects stick around to feast on aphids, caterpillar eggs, and spider mites. Basil, marigolds, and borage all help keep your garden pest-free and organic. Borage also has pretty blue and pink flowers which attract bees and aid in the pollination process.

Old deacon's or church benches make attractive garden benches. Old cream cans can become country treasures. They can be sponge painted, stenciled, or even painted in a solid color. They look great on decks or patios…and don't forget a raffia bow for extra measure!

★ ★ ★ ★ ★ ★ ★ ★ ★ ★ ★ ★ ★ ★ ★ ★ ★

A wall or freestanding fountain in the garden offers a relaxing atmosphere for reading or dreaming. It also encourages the birds to swim and bathe, and their melodic chirps make quite a symphony for your own "Secret Garden!"

★ ★ ★ ★ ★ ★ ★ ★ ★ ★ ★ ★ ★ ★ ★ ★ ★

Any country garden comes to life when surrounded, even on one side, by a white picket fence with climbing roses and posts topped with birdhouses. Set a tall post on one end of your garden with a purple martin house. It adds just the perfect country touch!

Pick herbs often to promote bushier plants.

I have enjoyed developing a perennial bed over the years and have found it helpful to draw a "floor plan" of where everything has been planted. With this plan sheet I include the color and type of perennial that I have planted. Even when markers are placed by the plant, they tend to get lost or destroyed; so each year when plants begin to sprout I know which ones are flowers and which are not. I have mistakenly pulled out sprouting plants without knowing what they were. This plan makes for easy identification in future years. Also, if something doesn't come up the following year, I know what to replace.

CORN

TOMATO

PEAS

PEPPER

Close your eyes and listen
to the sounds of nature...
crickets chirping, doves cooing,
geese honking, bees buzzing.
It's quite a performance,
and it's all for free!

A charming way to bring "country" to your garden
and to keep your favorite gardener organized, is
to mount a mailbox to a wood post and place it in
your garden. The "garden box" is a handy catch-all
for gardening supplies...gloves, tools, etc. The box
is easy to paint and is cute with watermelons, sunflowers or pumpkins adorning its sides. A grapevine
wreath mounted to
the wood post adds
charm to your
country garden
as well.

Save any flower garden catalogs you get through
the mail, even though you may not be planning to
send an order. They are great for future referral,
when you do want to plan a flower bed. They usually
list the name, color, size, sun/shade
requirements, and growth habits of
plants you may be interested in. These
catalogs sometimes also include exam-
ples of professionally planned gardens.
Many of the plants shown can be found
at a large nursery or garden center.

Water deeply once or twice a week
to encourage stronger roots and help
sustain the plant in dry periods.

Garden Themes

Butterfly Garden

The secret to attracting butterflies is to give them what they like to eat and drink! Use large splashes of color in your design; butterflies at first are attracted to color. Many seem to like purple, yellow, orange, and red flowers. Plant in groups, which are easier for butterflies to locate than isolated plants. Also, plant single rather than double type flowers; the nectar is more accessible. Sun is also very important to the life of these plants. Your first choice for a butterfly garden should be the shrub *buddleia davidii* (butterfly bush). The following flowers are also successful: zinnia, globe amaranth, verbena, lantana marigold, cosmos (bright lights), butterfly weed, lavender, purple coneflower, yarrow, and the New England aster. Tucking in some plants where their young can feed will encourage butterflies to stay. Caterpillars will nibble their way through milkweed, clover, nettle, Queen Anne's lace, wild lupine, and goldenrod. They also like garden plants such as carrots, dill, parsley, nasturtium, and violets.

When butterflies aren't searching for food, they like to rest on sun-warmed stones or boards. They prefer direct sunlight and heat. If you live in a windy area, plant your garden in a spot protected from exposed areas...next to a building or evergreen hedge. They also get thirsty. Fill a shallow pan with water and place it slightly in the ground in your garden.

A favorite of both butterflies and hummingbirds is the Mexican sunflower. These bloom in August with a bright orange and red color, and grow to about 3 or 4 feet tall. The stems feel like velvet and the flowers are 1 to 2 inches wide. They are an annual, but you can collect the seeds for use the next year.

Hummingbird Garden

For a hummingbird garden (a butterfly garden is a perfect companion) use tubular, brightly colored flowers. Because hummingbirds rely on sight to locate food, fragrance is not important. Like butterflies, hummingbirds prefer single flowers to doubles, and require a continuous supply of nectar. Plant flowers that bloom over a long season, like salvia, lobelia, monarda (bee balm), and trumpet vine. To make hummingbird nectar, mix one part granulated sugar to four parts water. First boil the water; then add the sugar, stirring to dissolve thoroughly. Let the solution cool. Store unused solution in the refrigerator.

A shallow birdbath kept clean, and filled with fresh water every day is an essential part of your "bird garden." Dripping or trickling water has a special appeal and will attract species you ordinarily might not see.

Moonlight Gardens

Here are some plants that will shimmer in the moonlight and add a lovely contrast to the darker foliage in your garden.

aloe • lamb's ears • silver sage • silver tansy • silver thyme • southernwood • wormwood • yarrow • apple mint • lavender • carnation • geranium • oregano • nutmeg • rosemary • horehound silver • silver king • artemisia • queen artemisia • germander • dwarf sage • pineapple mint • gray santolina • clary sage

Wildflower Garden

Gather plants and wildflowers from the fields and woods near your home. Wild ginger, violets, wild geraniums, daylilies, daisies, black-eyed Susans, irises, bee balm, yarrow, and Queen Anne's lace are just a few of the "country cousins" that can grow happily beside more "cultivated" neighbors. Not only are these lovely ladies easy on your budget, but they're indigenous to your area and grow readily in your garden. Enjoy your gathering walks, taking along a shovel, plastic bags with handles, a wildflower identification book, and a special friend.

Kitchen Garden

A snip of this and a snip of that right by your kitchen door!

basil • rosemary • marjoram • dill • parsley • savory • tarragon • sage • oregano • thyme • chives

EDIBLE FLOWERS:

all culinary herbs • scented geraniums • bachelor's button • snapdragon • begonia • tulip • calendula (petals) • viola • cornflower • violet • fuchsia • dandelion (petals) • gladiolus

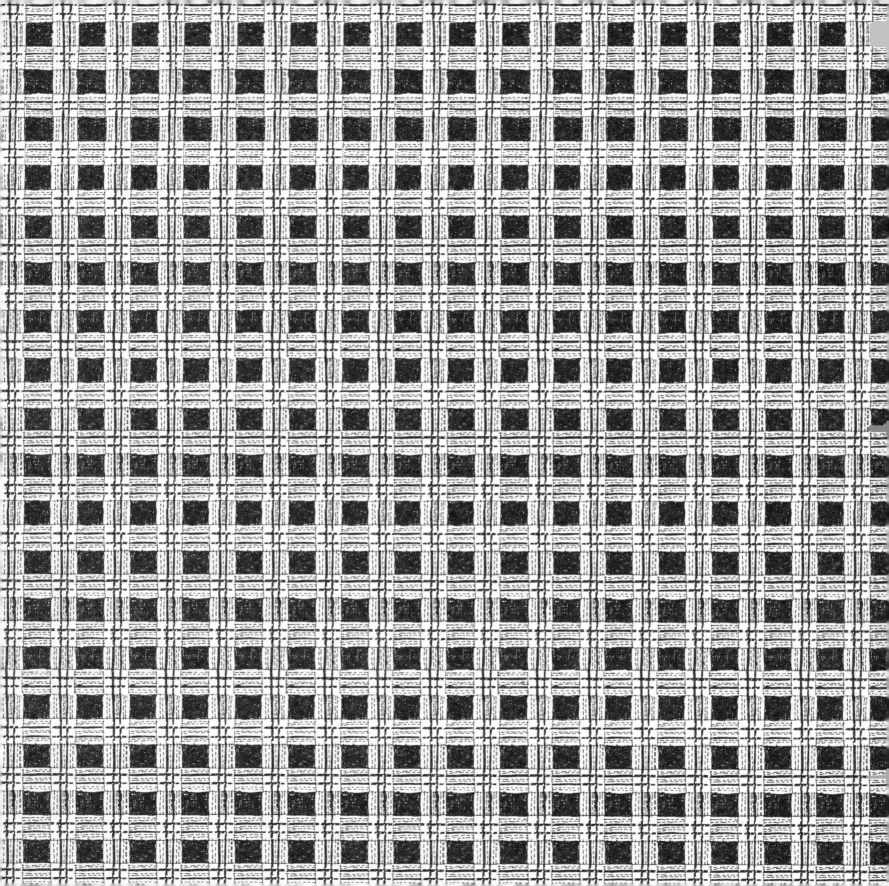

chapter three **The HerBaL PantRY**

Tarragon Cider Vinegar

About Herbs

Herbs need protection from wind, as it does more damage than low temperatures. A protected corner...near a wall, hedge, or a natural slope... can provide good shelter. Once the garden is established, the larger herbs will provide protection for the smaller ones.

There are several factors to consider when deciding where best to locate your herb garden. Many herbs have their origin in warmer climates. You want to reproduce, as nearly as possible, the conditions of their native habitat. Six to eight hours of sun a day is required to develop the essential oils which give plants their fragrance and flavor. Even plants that require partial shade need up to four hours of sun.

My mother and I correspond back and forth, and we always close our letters with: "P.S. My 'thyme' with you is a pleasure." I like to include a sprig of garden thyme and lemon thyme between the pages.

Herbs That Are Fun to Grow

Borage, the herb of courage, was smuggled into the drink of prospective suitors to give them courage to propose marriage. Finely chopped young leaves mixed with cream cheese makes a nice tea sandwich. The leaves have a cucumber-like flavor and can be added to salads. Or, add leaves and flowers to fruit salad. The pretty blue starlike flowers can be candied and used for accents on cakes or ice cream. Add a crushed leaf to your favorite summer drink. Dry the leaves for a winter tea.

Lavender is the herb of devotion and undying love and it has always been associated with washing. In olden days, lavender was added to rinse water for a clean fresh scent, or newly washed clothes were spread over lavender bushes to dry. Victorian ladies made lavender wands and placed

> Lavender will sweeten linens and soothe the soul. Add a few dried lavender spikes to drawers and closets.

them among their fine linens. Put a sprig of lavender under your hat to drive away a headache.

Peppermint spreads like crazy and in the spring you can make lots of little plants to share. Just pull up a piece of your plant along with the root. It will come up easily. Put it in little pots and give it away.

Parsley. The symbol of strength and vigor, parsley is a popular kitchen herb. It's a hardy biennial, often grown as an annual. Italian parsley leaves are flat while French parsley leaves are curly. It does best in rich soil with full sun. While it can be grown from seed, it takes about four weeks to germinate and is sometimes more reliable when grown from small plants. Garnish your summertime dishes with parsley, a rich source of vitamins and minerals. It is especially good in potatoes and rice.

Basil is a wonderful herb to plant in the garden because it is easy to grow, attracts honeybees, goes great with tomatoes (both in cuisine and as a companion planting), and smells great when you brush up against it as you tend your garden. Plant lettuce-leaf basil for making pesto and other recipes in which large quantities of basil are needed, but don't forget other varieties such as the purple basils (beautiful in salads), the miniature and globe-shaped basil, lemon basil, and Thai basil, which are fun to use in salads and other cuisine.

Chives taste wonderful cut up and sprinkled over baked potatoes. But have you tried them in your scrambled eggs, potato salad, macaroni salad, and fresh green salads? Yummy! Use the blossoms…the lovely pink and lavender adds color to a wildflower and herb bouquet. The scent is pleasing too. Blossoms can be cut and dried upside down (about two to three weeks) and then used in dried flower arrangements or tucked into wreaths.

Rosemary means "dew of the sea." It is the herb of friendship and remembrance and is considered the herb of Christmas, weddings, and

chives

rosemary

sage

Herb Garden

thyme

parsley

sandy soil in full sun to about 6 to 10 inches high, and has pink or violet flowers in the early fall. If you plant thyme between rocks in your garden path, you'll delight in its heavenly fragrance every time you pass. It's best to start with tiny plants as seeds are slow to germinate. Thyme is used in poultry stuffings and as a seasoning for chicken and pot roast.

Spearmint is easy to grow and spreads everywhere! Use leaves in ice molds, or throw a stem in when you brew sun tea. Freeze some in a resealable plastic sandwich bag and save for hot tea in the winter. Or, try drying some leaves and keep them in a jar. Around Christmas time, add to the pot-pourri pot or make a dry potpourri

funerals. For weddings, rosemary was either gilded or dipped in scented water and carried in the bride's bouquet. It is said that where rosemary flourishes, the woman rules. Dried twigs and leaves thrown on the coals of a wood stove or fireplace make a natural incense, and in days of old, were used this way to clear the air in a sick room.

Thyme. There are several varieties of thyme...lemon, creeping, and common. A perennial herb, it's a favorite of bees! It grows in dry,

The heart that loves is always young.
—Greek proverb

sachet. It also makes a great garnish. A few sprigs of leaves with a few fresh strawberries look nice on the top of a chocolate cake (or vanilla, if you prefer). And when someone has a cold, put it in a pot of hot water (where little hands can't reach it) and let the minty smell fill the air.

Sweet Annie. Buy your plants or start from seed in early spring. Give it plenty of room to grow and lots of sun. When seedheads form in late fall, cut and dry branches upside down. Leave some branches to self-sow. Use sweet Annie to make wreaths, swags, or add to any dried floral arrangement. The fragrance is exquisite!

Tarragon, a member of the anise family, is indispensable to

French cuisine. It is a perennial in most areas and likes a sunny and well-drained spot in the garden. Protect in winter with mulch. Tarragon can also be grown indoors or outdoors in pots. Use it fresh or dried in recipes. Tarragon vinegar is delicious in salad dressings. It is also excellent with chicken, mayonnaise, fish, and egg dishes.

Sage was a sacred herb in medieval times used for healing. Today, sage is prized as a culinary herb and is excellent with all poultry, pork, and apple baked goods. Sage is also used in potpourris, wreaths, and nosegays. It retains a lot of scent, even when dried. Sage prefers full sun and good drainage in the garden or in pots. There are many varieties including gold, purple, and variegated colors. Some plants stay small; others grow to large, aromatic shrubs.

> Neither a lofty degree of intelligence nor imagination nor both together go to the making of genius. Love, love, love, that is the soul of genius.
> —Wolfgang Amadeus Mozart

Herbs & Beauty

Calendula. An all-around skin herb, calendula softens, nourishes and cleanses the skin, heals minor irritations, and reduces pores and thread veins. Use it in cleansing lotions, facial steams, and baths. As a shampoo or rinse, it highlights blonde or brown hair.

Chamomile. Slightly astringent, the Roman variety soothes and cleanses in facial steams, baths, and face masks. In a lotion, it softens and keeps skin young and firm. When used as shampoo or rinse, it softens and adds highlights to blonde or brown hair.

Comfrey. Healing and slightly astringent, it soothes and moisturizes dry skin and can also be used in baths, face packs, and facial steams. It is said to regenerate aging skin.

Fennel. Both the leaves and seeds can be used in a slightly astringent skin tonic, cleansing lotion, and face pack. Fennel lotion guards against wrinkles, and a poultice will reduce puffiness around the eyes.

Lady's Mantle. Healing and slightly astringent, it is good for dry skin in facial steams and packs. A lotion will refine large pores, minimize freckles, and reduce inflammations. There is an old saying that if you drink of the dew found on the leaves on the first day following a full moon in June, the next fellow you see will be your true love (you must partake of this dew in the nude!).

Lemon geranium leaves added to your bath water scents the whole bathroom as you bathe and smells heavenly.

To give your sheets a fresh scent of lavender, place a washcloth sprinkled with a few drops of lavender oil into your wash.

Lavender. Lavender water refines pores and is good for oily skin. Its antiseptic qualities make it helpful for acne. It also reduces puffiness, is stimulating for the hair, and adds a lovely fragrance to the bath.

Lemon Balm. Soothing and astringent, a lotion of lemon balm is said to act against wrinkles. It is a gentle cleanser in lotions and baths and adds a delicious fragrance to everything. Lemon balm is good for lifting the spirits.

Marjoram. Joy, happiness, kindness. It was used to crown young married couples in Greek and Roman days, and brought to America by the colonists in 1640. Mildly antiseptic and stimulating.

Nettle. Eat the young leaves like spinach to improve the complexion. Good for oily skin, it is cleansing and stimulates circulation in facial steams and baths. Use in shampoo for healthier hair or as a rinse to condition and prevent dandruff.

Parsley. Good for oily skin. Adds shine to dark hair when used as a rinse. A lotion reduces freckles and thread veins. A great source of Vitamins A and C.

Peppermint. Healing and astringent, it's stimulating in facial steams and masks. It's also an invigorating and cooling bath herb for hot summer days.

Rose. Lightly astringent, rose water cleanses and refreshes skin, and acts as a hydrating agent to help keep it young looking. Mix rose water and glycerin for a soothing lotion for chapped hands. Refreshing and fragrant in the bath.

Rosemary. Good for oily skin. Invigorating in the bath or in facial steams. Use in a shampoo or rinse to give dark hair body and shine, and keep it healthy.

Thyme. Deodorizing, antiseptic, and makes a good tonic for the bath. A lotion is good for cleansing and reducing spots and pimples. Soothing and gentle.

Yarrow. Quite astringent. Used for oily skin in face packs and facial steams. Cleansing in the bath and in a lotion. Helps thread veins and stimulates hair growth. Healing herb for oily skin. In Old England, a little pillow stuffed with yarrow was said to produce a dream vision of a young girl's future husband when placed under her pillow.

Herbal Steam

2 c. fresh herbs or 1 c. dried herbs
Hot (not boiling) water

Place herbs in a bowl, add hot water, and stir well. Drape a towel over your head to trap the steam, and steam your face for 5 minutes.

Herbal Facial Pack

2 T. plain yogurt
2 T. herb leaves selected according to skin type, finely chopped
1 to 2 T. fine oatmeal
1 to 2 t. lemon juice (optional)

Stir the yogurt and herbs together until well-blended. Stir in enough oatmeal to form a soft paste and mix well. If you have acne or oily skin, you may want to add one to 2 teaspoons of lemon juice to the mixture. For storage, spoon paste into a jar, cover, label, and store in the refrigerator.

Scented Floral Water

32 oz. distilled water
¼ oz. rose oil

Combine distilled water and rose oil in a jar. Shake well and let steep for one week. Transfer to decorative bottles after steeping. Interesting old bottles can be found at yard sales, flea markets, etc. Rose water is said to be good for strengthening of the heart and refreshing of the spirits.

Quick & Easy Herbal Lotion

Buy inexpensive, unscented lotion. Pick a small bundle of peppermint leaves from your garden and crush slightly. Add to unscented lotion and allow to sit undisturbed for a week. Transfer to a pretty jar and, if you like, store in your refrigerator. This will make a nice relaxing rub for tired feet!

Chamomile Hair Rinse

Place one cup of fresh or dried chamomile flowers in a large jug and pour in 3¾ cups of boiling water. Cover with a plate and leave until cool. Wash and rinse your hair as you would usually. Strain the chamomile infusion and use as a final rinse. A chamomile rinse is a good conditioner and brings out the highlights in blonde hair.

Fragrant Massage Oil

Relieve aching muscles with essential oils.

½ oz. olive oil
3 drops chamomile oil
3 drops birch oil
8 drops lavender oil
3 drops ginger oil
3 drops rosemary oil

Combine all oils and massage into tense muscles after a warm bath.

Sleep Pillow

lemon balm or lemon clove
verbena
cinnamon
catnip or marjoram
lavender
chamomile

Be sure all the ingredients are completely dry before combining them, then store in a tightly sealed container in a cool, dark place for four or five days. Use one or two of the sedative varieties mentioned above as a base, then add rose petals or leaves, mint, any of the lemon-scented herbs, linden blossoms, or any favorite herb or spice for fragrance. Once you've decided on the blend, you're ready to make the bag itself. It should be flat, even after it's filled, so it is comfortable to lie on, and not too large; or make one for the bedpost. Seam three sides of a rectangle, pink the top, then tie on with satin ribbon.

Using Sleep Pillows:
1. Even babies can benefit. A sleep pillow filled with dill (an herb seldom used for adults) will lull them to sleep when they're restless.
2. Stitch one up in muslin and keep it handy to insert in a pillowcase or small boudoir pillow.
3. If sewing isn't your forte, simply fill the center of a lacy handkerchief, gather the corners, and wrap up with ribbon.
4. Keep your herb pillow nearby for an hour or so before you go to bed, then either sleep on it, or keep it close to your head. Enjoy the gentle fragrance as you drift off and slip into the sweetest of dreams.

Window Garden

Create a romantic atmosphere in your bedroom by planting a fragrant garden outside your window. This can be accomplished for a first or second floor room by using window boxes and certain varieties of climbing plants. Allow the runners from climbing plants to encircle the window. Some favorites are wisteria, clematis, jasmine, gardenia, and some antique roses. When spring arrives, open your window to enjoy the soothing scents.

Tie a bunch of lavender to your shower head and enjoy the fragrance as you shower.

Herb Soap Balls

Cut up 3 bars of white soap and 2 bars of green into small pieces. Pour 1½ cups of boiling water over 2 teaspoons of an aromatic herb (sage, mint, thyme, rosemary, lavender, chamomile, bergamot, or anise). Allow to steep for a few minutes and then strain out herbs (I often leave them in the soap) and pour mixture over cut-up soap pieces. Mix well with your hands (wait until cool enough to handle). Soap chips should be moist, not "swimming." Set aside for approximately 15 minutes, or until mixture is mushy. Mix softened soap again and divide into 5 parts. Place one part onto a piece of muslin or flannel; cheesecloth will also work. These squares of fabric should be approximately 8 inches. Using your hands, form soap into balls. Pull cloth tightly around soap ball, gather at the top, and tie with string or pretty ribbon. Hang soap balls to dry in a warm place. This will take approximately 3 days. Soap is dry when it is completely hard. Unwrap and use, or give as a gift by wrapping in a pretty fabric with a ribbon! Kids and adults alike can enjoy this project, and reap the benefits as well...a luxurious bath! You can combine aromatic herbs and spices for all kinds of wonderful scents. It's good clean fun and can be a downright artistic endeavor if you care to experiment. I like to tie a small bundle of dried herbs into the ribbon on the soap ball...it makes a small, but lovely gift.

Herbal Bath Bags

Stimulate and delight your body with the joy of herbal baths! Herbal baths can relax and calm you, revive and stimulate you, ease aching limbs, or help a tired circulation. Shower first, giving your entire body a thorough soaping and rinsing. Hang your herbal bath bag under the faucet as you draw a warm bath. Now, turn on your favorite music, reach for a good book, get a pillow for under your head, and step into your herbal bath. Relax and enjoy!

Herbal Hair Rinse

For dark hair…one part strong rosemary tea and four parts water.

For light hair…one part strong chamomile tea and four parts water. Pour over washed hair, catching water, and repeating until rinse is used up.

Easy Dusting Powder

One part dried herbs or 4 parts cornstarch flowers, finely ground

Just find a little jar or box, add puff, and tie with a pretty bow.

Herbal Bath Vinegar

Cider vinegar added to the bath will soften skin. Fill a glass jar halfway with chopped fresh herbs. Pour cider vinegar over the herbs to fill jar. Cover and place in a sunny window for 3 weeks. Strain off the vinegar and add an equal amount of spring water. Put in a clean jar and leave for one week. Another method is to heat one cup spring water and one cup vinegar to just below the boiling point in a nonmetal pan. Pour in a jar that is half full of chopped fresh herbs. Cover and leave for 12 hours. Strain and bottle. Shake well. To use as bath vinegars, add 1 cup to bath water while running. Victorian ladies wore tiny bottles of herb and floral vinegars around their necks.

"REMEMBER WHEN..." BATH

To refresh the memory and bring out the child in you...place one cup of rosemary and one cup peppermint leaves in a nonmetal pan filled with water and bring to a boil. Lower heat and simmer for 10 minutes. Strain and pour into bath water. Put on your favorite music, light some candles, lay back, relax, close your eyes, and remember those carefree days of your childhood. Enjoy!

Herb & Flower Splash

Place 6 tablespoons of chopped fresh herbs and one pint of spring water in a nonmetal pan and bring to a gentle boil. Cover and simmer for 20 minutes. Cool completely, strain and put in a bottle. A spray bottle works wonderfully. Keep in your refrigerator during the warm months; it will keep up to 2 weeks. Rosemary, lavender, and peppermint are especially refreshing. Search for unusual bottles for these herbal delights. If you have a plain bottle, make little flower wreaths for around the necks of the bottles or tie with fancy French ribbons.

Herb and flower splashes are great when you feel tired and sluggish. Keep in the bedroom or bath. They replenish moisture in your skin, and are great to keep in the bedroom or bath. Rose, lavender, and thyme are refreshing and fragrant, while chamomile and lemon balm are soothing. Herb and flower splashes should be left to dry on your skin.

For the Home

Birdbath End Table

This table will add some summer whimsy to your sunroom or screened-in porch.

plaster birdbath
foam paintbrush
¼" glass to fit birdbath
trim roller
dark green latex paint
dried flowers,
    seashells
white staining
    glaze
colorful stones

Measure the width of the birdbath bowl just below the lip, and have glass cut to fit. Paint the birdbath with green paint and let dry. Use the roller to apply white glaze over the entire birdbath, highlighting the texture. When dry, fill the bowl with an arrangement of flowers, shells, or stones, and place glass on top.

Floral Spoons

Collect pretty, deep-bowled spoons and ladles from flea markets to make this easy craft. They make beautiful party favors!

old spoons
florist's foam
tacky craft glue
thin satin ribbon
    small dried flower blossoms such as
      purple statice, baby's breath, globe
      amaranth, and lavender

Cut a small amount of florist's foam to fill the well of the spoon. (A melon baller works perfectly to cut the foam for a regular tablespoon.) Glue foam firmly into the spoon and let dry completely, overnight if possible. When dry, push dried flowers into the base, completely covering the foam. Tie a bow onto the spoon handle.

Canning Jar Potpourri

These "jarred" potpourri collections make beautiful gifts any time of year. Layer the ingredients for a nice effect. Make your own labels and paste on for a truly personalized touch.

several old canning jars
2 T. ground cinnamon
1 T. ground cloves
dried mint leaves
sandalwood chips
mixed herb leaves
dried marigold petals
cedar chips or shavings
    (available at pet stores)
lavender
scented oil
dried tea roses, peonies,
    and hydrangeas
sheets of paper to use as
    funnels

Combine cinnamon and cloves and place on the bottom of the jar. Layer scant cupfuls of ingredients in the following order: mint leaves, sandalwood chips, herbs, marigold, cedar chips, lavender, marigold, sandalwood, and oil. Complete the jar by adding dried flowers and petals and more oil before placing lid on jar. To use, leave jar open or put a scrap of netting or fabric over the opening, secured with a canning jar ring.

> We all need a little time and space devoted to our own well-being. We can give so much more to others when we've given to ourselves.

Recipe Cards and Holder

A family reunion is a great time to catch up, have fun, and enjoy family cooking! Someone is going to ask for a favorite recipe…it always happens…so this time, be prepared. Make some recipe cards and holders for each family. They're quick, easy, and sure to be a hit.

scraps of coordinating fabrics
tracing paper
giant clothespins
    (you can find 7"
    clothespins at
    most craft stores)
pinking shears
craft glue
3" × 5" index cards
marking pen

Make 2 hearts—one smaller than the other, trace onto tracing paper, and cut out. Place heart patterns on fabric and draw around outline. Use pinking shears to cut the hearts out of the fabric. Cut out 3 large hearts for each recipe holder, and as many smaller hearts as you wish to decorate the recipe cards. Glue large hearts vertically onto the clothespin, one above the other. Glue small hearts onto the back of each index card. Tie a bundle of recipe cards together with jute and clip with the clothespin to give to relatives.

Note: You can use this idea with other designs…for instance, you might want to use the initial of your family name instead of a heart pattern.

Decorated Trays

Here's a fun and functional gift that everyone will love to take home. Découpage small unfinished wooden trays with old seed packs and labels. Use the trays as place settings, along with small notebooks and pencils for garden planning. They make lunch more portable and will serve as a charming remembrance of your garden party.

Apple Candles

You'll need 12 or 13 apples and the same number of tea lights or votive candles, plus a lemon. Cut a thin slice off the bottom of each apple so it will stand upright. Core each apple, widening the space to accommodate a tea light or votive. Sprinkle lemon juice on the apple to keep it from turning brown. Insert your candles and light.

Ivy Topiary

A lovely idea to brighten your living room.

heavy-gauge wire
wire cutter
needle-nose pliers
small pebbles
6" terra-cotta pot
potting soil
2 small ivy plants
twine

Cut a strand of wire about 3 feet long. Bend the wire into a circle and use pliers to twist the ends together. The end piece should be about 5 inches long, or long enough to reach the bottom of the pot. Shape the loop into a circle. Put pebbles into the bottom of the pot, fill it halfway with potting soil, and plant your ivies in the center. Make sure the shoots are growing outward in opposite directions. Cover the plants with additional soil and tap the pot to settle the roots. Water generously, allowing excess water to drain. Place your wire topiary form in the pot between the plants so it is firmly in the soil. Gently wrap the shoots around the twisted wire and onto both sides of the form. Temporarily tie the shoots in place with small pieces of twine. Then watch your topiary grow!

> Turn a watering can or birdhouse into a country lamp. Just purchase a lamp-conversion kit, drill a hole for the cord, and install. It's easy and your friends will rave.

Herbal Calendar Box

A kind and thoughtful gift that can be made for as little or as much money as you choose, by putting your own special brand of creativity to work. A lovely gift for either a gardener or a cook.

pretty 4" × 6" file box
4" × 6" cards
12 plain subject 3" × 5" index cards
seeds

1. Write the months of the year on the 12 index cards.
2. Buy pretty packets of herbal seeds for each month of the year. Place these seeds in file box according to suitable planting times. In cold climates where some months may be inappropriate for planting outside, include seeds that can be started indoors with instructions on how to start seeds indoors. In cold climates when even starting seed indoors would be ill-advised, give a gift certificate from a local nursery or florist for an indoor flowering herb, plant, or perhaps some bulbs like paperwhite or narcissus, to be planted in pots and forced for indoor blooming.
3. Decide which month your seeds would be ready to harvest and write recipes for using that herb. File under the proper month.
4. All kinds of gardening information can be included for the proper month, depending on the expertise of your cook or gardener.
5. File box can be decorated with paint or contact paper in garden tool, or kitchen tool design; or simply tied with a pretty bow.

Wreath in Bloom

This wreath is great for showcasing the prettiest blossoms from your garden. It's also pretty with silk flowers when your garden isn't blooming.

1. Attach a hanging loop to a grapevine wreath.
2. Attach floral wire securely around the neck of several small bottles. (Probably five, depending on size of wreath.) Baby food or spice bottles work well.
3. Wire bottles to wreath at evenly spaced intervals, leaving a space at the top for a bow. You may wish to further secure the bottles to the wreath with hot glue.
4. Cover the wiring with ribbon bows. Add streamers as you wish.
5. Add a bow at the top of the wreath. You might want to put the bow on a floral pick to make it easier to change.
6. Add water to bottles, fill with bouquets of fresh flowers, greenery, and baby's breath. (Water can be removed with a meat baster or a small sponge.)

Seed Packet Magnets

Fill empty seed packets with Spanish moss and a tiny homemade or store-bought muslin bunny. Then glue a magnet on back! You can also use them to decorate a wreath.

Fresh Floral Lampshade

Decorate an old, tired lampshade with fabric. Cut flowers out of a pretty floral cotton fabric. Apply craft glue to the flowers and press them onto the shade in a pleasing pattern.

Country Swag

Decorate a wall or fence with this easy country swag. You will need quite a few bay leaves, several mini terra-cotta pots with small holes drilled on each side, a mini watering can, and strong jute or twine. String the bay leaves and pots alternately, with the watering can in the middle. Use homespun fabric strips or ribbon to tie on whatever you choose.

> Be sure to display finished projects in a scrapbook or on the refrigerator. Some creations even deserve framing. You'll treasure them over the years!

Sunflower Wreaths

What do you do with all those sunflower heads at the end of the growing season? Turn them into wreaths for the birds! Just before the heads get too dry, cut them from the stem as close to the head as possible. Then cut a hole in the very center (you'll have a donut shape!). When they are dry, make a small bouquet of millet, wheat, and other autumnal foliage. Glue gun or wire it on the sunflower wreath. Using string or raffia, hang the wreath outside where you (and the birds!) can enjoy it. Makes a great gift as well!

Pressed–Flower Candle

Gather an assortment of pressed flowers and leaves, a small white votive candle, and a white pillar candle. Melt the votive candle in the top of a double boiler. Working quickly, apply melted wax to the back of a pressed flower with an artist's brush. Place the flower immediately onto the pillar candle. Cover the flowers with another thin coat of wax to set.

Herbal Candle Ring

An easy craft idea for your tabletop. Start with a wreath base made of floral foam. Cover the base with Spanish moss, using floral pins to hold it in place. Attach floral picks to small bundles of dried sweet Annie and arrange the bunches around the wreath's inner and outer rims. Fill in the middle with more dried herbs and flowers. Choose from white and pink statice, larkspur, lavender, everlasting, oregano, and roses. Spray the wreath with a commercial fixative. Place a pillar candle in the middle.

Pansy Frame

Frame your favorite photo in this romantic, ribbon-covered frame. Choose a plain wooden frame with a glass insert. Select a roll of pretty florist's wired ribbon. Using small accordion folds, cover the frame with ribbon all the way around, overlapping the ribbon in staggered 1-inch folds. Secure the ribbon onto the frame with dots of hot glue. Place pressed, dried pansies on the ribbon with hot glue. Add a few random petals among the pansies.

Unique Lamps

Turn almost any unique item into a lamp. The most fun is hunting for old watering cans, crocks, tins, teapots, and such. Simple lamp-making kits can be found at most hardware stores. My favorite lamp is one I made from an old watering can. I découpaged a vintage seed packet on the front and added a lampshade covered with seed packet design fabric. Inexpensive plain white lampshades can be found at discount stores for a song and covered with whatever fabric you like. Spray adhesive makes it simple.

Fragrance Logs

Combine lavender, dill, sage, and scented geraniums. Roll into small compact bundles and tie with raffia. May be tied into a fragrant wall hanging by the fireplace. Toss them in a crackling fire for a wonderful fragrance!

Angels in the early morning
May be seen the dews among,
Stooping, plucking, smiling, flying.
Do the buds to them belong?
—Emily Dickinson

Garlands

Anyone who enjoys making wreaths and working with flowers will really love trying a garland. It adds a touch of spring and sweet fragrance to your hearth. There are so many different types of garlands to make. The following are a few suggestions. Remember, if you're drying fruits (apples or oranges) you can use three methods: screen, dehydrator, or oven. Apples and oranges need to be sliced thin, but not paper thin. Spread in a single layer.

Screen drying: Place screen in the warm sun or in an attic. No humidity is a must...it will ruin the fruit! This method can take two weeks or longer.

Oven drying: Set the oven at less than 200°. Slices must be turned and checked, and the oven door must be slightly open for air circulation. Apples will generally take 8 to 10 hours; oranges are quicker, sometimes drying in only 2 hours. Both should be leathery to the touch. Keep the heat low and don't try and rush the results with higher heat...it will spoil the color, causing the fruits to turn brown.

Dehydrator: This is a terrific method because it's energy efficient and you can control the heat and air circulation. With the heat set at the highest setting, apple slices will dry in 8 to 12 hours, oranges will look their best if dried at a lower temperature and

given more time. For a dehydrator or oven, the trick is to set a timer and constantly check them until they are tough and leathery to the touch. If they're too dry, they'll be brittle; and if they're too soft, they'll spoil! It sounds difficult, but it's not. Just keep checking...and be patient.

Stringing: This is the fun part! You'll need thin twine or fishing line, and a large-eyed tapestry needle. Decide how long you'd like your garland and remember to cut your twine 6 to 8 inches longer to allow for a knots at the ends. Tie a loop at one end of the string and secure it with a knot. Then thread the other end of the string through the needle. The idea is to puncture your material and gently push them onto the string.

You can string all kinds of goodies on your garland...fruits, bay leaves, nuts (will need a hole drilled in them first), everlastings, cinnamon sticks, pinecones, Indian corn, or pomegranates (holes drilled here, too). The list goes on! Roses are beautiful or try black-eyed Susans for a more country look. They will stay fresh for a day or two, or let them dry. Slip your materials over the twine, carefully pushing them close together. When you're finished, remove the needle, tie another loop, and knot securely. Hang and enjoy!

> **Treat yourself to an adventure. Do something you've never done before! Visit a new town and explore the shops...take dancing, swimming, or painting lessons... go mushroom hunting...go on a retreat. An adventure can renew your spirits and awaken your senses. You'll feel refreshed and vibrant.**

For Your Garden

Braided Bird Wreath

Make a picnic for the birds…they'll flock to this summertime treat, and you'll enjoy watching the birds in your backyard.

1 lb. frozen bread dough, thawed
1 egg
½ c. wild birdseed

Grease the outside of a 9" round cake pan and place on a greased cookie sheet. Roll out dough into a 30" rope. Using a sharp knife, cut the dough into thirds lengthwise and braid. Place braided dough around the outside of the cake pan and seal the edges by pinching them together. Cover with a clean dish towel and let rise 30 minutes, or until double in size. Bake in a pre-heated 375° oven for 20 minutes. While bread is baking, whisk egg in a small bowl. Remove bread from the oven, brush with egg, sprinkle with birdseed and bake 10 minutes longer. Remove from the pan and let set for 24 hours uncovered. Hang outside for the birds to enjoy!

Weathered Clay Pot Planters

These planters are so easy, and they look great potted with a variety of cactus plants, Mexican heather, or herbs. Just rub the outside of new clay pots with buttermilk. Let them stand for three weeks in a shaded, damp area like a garage or basement. They'll look like they've been around since the pioneers settled the Old West!

Country Garden Birdbath

Make a country garden birdbath by using an old porch post and an old granite dishpan. Cut an old (or new) porch post off to approximately 4 feet. Place post in the ground so that it is buried at least one foot and stands securely. Screw your dish pan into the center of the top of the post. Surround with country flowers.

Garden Markers

Begin with wooden hearts found at a craft store. Paint desired color and allow to dry. Print flower or herb name onto heart, and let dry. Sand lightly to give an aged look. Glue a large craft stick on back for a stake to place in a flowerpot or flower bed.

My garden of Herbs of

**We know nothing of tomorrow; our business is to be good and happy today.
—Sydney Smith**

Terrarium

**glass container like a fishbowl
bits of charcoal
small pebbles
natural soil
plastic bags
spade or large spoon**

Making a terrarium is a good camping project for kids. First, be sure plant collecting is allowed where you'll be camping…get permission if necessary. Pack a glass container to hold your terrarium…a large fishbowl or wide-mouthed mayonnaise jar are perfect. Put a layer of charcoal on the bottom (plain charcoal briquettes work very well). The charcoal will keep your terrarium from decaying. Next, put a layer of pebbles over the charcoal. They will help the water to drain away from the roots of the plants. The next layer is soil, which you can get from wherever the plants are growing. Collect tiny plants that grow near one another, because these are the ones that will do well in the terrarium. With a large spoon and some plastic bags, collect mosses, miniature ferns, myrtle, wintergreen, and false lily of the valley. (You may want to look these plants up so you'll be able to recognize them.) Dig the plants as deeply and as gently as you can, keeping the roots intact. Plant as soon as possible. Water them and press them firmly into the soil. Put the moss in last to form a carpet. Add a few pretty stones to make a little woodland scene. Keep your terrarium in a spot where it will get some light, and water once a week with a spray bottle. The glass container will act as a greenhouse, keeping the plants moist and warm.

Garden Glove Decorations

Paint or stencil a design (using acrylic paints) on the back of an inexpensive pair of muslin garden gloves. How about a slice of watermelon, a sunflower, or even a ladybug? Stuff with or attach a matching packet of seeds. Tie together with raffia. You could even fill with birdseed. Hang indoors for a unique decoration!

Weathered Garden Signs

Any old weathered wood will work…barn siding, fence pickets…use your imagination! Hang sayings around yard or garden. A few hints:

"Never Enough Thyme"
"Thyme Began in a Garden"
"Thyme for Ewe" (this one would be cute for a spot in the garden just for yourself and no one else!)
"Thyme Will Tell"
"Please Touch the Herbs"
"Garden Sweet Garden"
"Garden of Weedin'"

Bird Cakes

You'll be able to attract birds to your garden all year round with these delicious treats. In the winter, birds really look forward to bird cakes. These can be kept in the freezer until ready to put out in a mesh bag or wire suet cage. The little clinging birds, like tufted titmice, chickadees, and woodpeckers, wait in line to get a bite. To make your own suet, save bacon drippings and chicken fat all year long. Keep in the freezer and melt down when ready to use. Ask friends to save some for you and in exchange give them some bird cakes for their yard. This also makes a nice gift for a bird watcher. Use festive muffin wrappers and gift tags.

1 part peanut butter
2 parts birdseed
5 parts cornmeal
12 parts melted suet

Melt suet and add to other ingredients in a large bowl. Mix with a wooden spoon. Line muffin cups with paper liners. Press mixture into cups and place in refrigerator until firm. Transfer to plastic bags and keep in freezer. Can also be kept in a cold garage or enclosed porch.

Hanging Wire Baskets

Hanging baskets have a variety of uses! Strawberries can trail over the edge of a hanging basket without letting the berries rot on the ground. Birds are discouraged from eating the ripe berries and picking couldn't be easier. How about an herb hanging basket? Plant several types of smaller herbs together in a hanging basket near the kitchen (or above the kitchen window!) and enjoy not just the convenience of a close-at-hand herb garden for cooking, but the relaxing scents of herbs closer to "nose" level. Try hanging an herbal basket in the bathroom, if there is adequate light (most herbs like lots of sun). Don't forget vegetables! Fresh cherry tomatoes in the winter grown in a hanging basket are such a treat. Grow different varieties of lettuce in a hanging basket...beautiful and tasty. Mix up your vegetables. Lettuce, radish, baby carrots, and a small marigold plant make a fun combination. Use your imagination. Remember that hanging baskets require lots of water, fertilizer, and sunshine. A watering wand is most handy for watering hanging gardens.

Line a wire basket with plenty of moss (you can buy moss at craft and garden stores). In the center of your basket put a pot or basket of well-established, small-sized plants. Caladiums will give good height. Fill in with soil and any kind of starter plants like begonias, impatiens, airplane plants, yew, and ivy; even small amounts of Boston fern. Add plants all around the baskets by pulling the wire and moss apart, pushing the plants into the soil, and then bending the wire back; even near the bottom of baskets it will all start to grow and the basket will be high and beautiful.

Stenciling adds a creative and charming country look to objects not only inside but outside your home. Using leftover outdoor paint and inexpensive stencil patterns, decorate the mailbox, flower boxes, around door and window frames, and even the porch steps! You can add little personal touches to the gate on the picket fence, a collection of terra-cotta flowerpots, and even accent a bird or dog house. When you decorate any of these items, the outside of your home will become unique and attractive.

Gifts

Personal Journal

Sometimes the demands of day-to-day living cause us to lose contact with our innermost thoughts and feelings. As a way of keeping in touch with yourself, consider recording your thoughts, dreams, and inspirations in a journal. Blank books are widely available in bookstores and stationery shops, some with elaborate and beautiful covers. Or, you can cover a regular notebook with fabric and glue, making the design your very own. Along with your thoughts, you can press flowers, paste in theater tickets, save special photographs. Keep a good-quality pen with your journal to encourage frequent writing. Journal writing is very satisfying in itself, and who knows? It may lead to an interesting biography one day!

Gift Coupon Book

Help the kids give Mom or Grandma a special book of coupons they've made just for her. Get out construction paper, magazines for picture cut-outs, markers, and glue. Help them think of things they can do for Mother's Day, like wash the dishes, clean the refrigerator, make dinner, go shopping, or weed the garden. Make each page into a "coupon" for the gift. (Include some coupons of your own if the gift is for your mother.)

this coupon good for: ONE DELICIOUS DINNER Cooked by Me!

this coupon good for: ONE WEED-FREE GARDEN (til they grow back)

Make a fairy teapot that is sure to delight every little girl (or the one inside of all us grown-up little girls)...a rosehip is the teapot, a thorn for the spout and a small twig for the handle. An acorn cup and saucer complete the set!

Lavender Pillow Sachets

Lavender lifts the spirits. You can grow your own lavender or purchase everything you need in an herb or craft shop.

2 c. dried lavender leaves
½ c. dried cornflowers
1½ t. orris root powder
1½ c. dried lavender buds
¾ c. dried juniper berries
8 drops lavender oil
4 drops rosemary oil
several 4-inch squares of fabric, needle, and thread

Combine all ingredients (except fabric, needle, and thread) in a glazed pottery bowl and cover tightly. Allow fragrances to blend and mellow for at least 2 weeks. Select muslin, calico, or homespun fabrics of your choice. Handstitch or sew 3 edges of 2 squares fitted together. Fill pouches with potpourri and sew remaining seams closed. Tuck these little "pillows" wherever you need a lift…inside your pillowcase, in your sweater drawer, in the linen closet. Make them as fancy as you wish with ribbon roses, lace, and appliqués. Make enough to give as gifts, or fill a pretty basket.

Tie your linens with a sachet-adorned ribbon and tuck in a fresh sprig of lavender to make them look and smell fresh and beautiful.

Butterfly Sachets

Stitch potpourri inside a double layer of scalloped eyelet material and tie tightly in the middle with a colorful narrow ribbon. Form a loop to hang on a door knob or in your closet. The potpourri will show through the eyelets in the material.

Floral Writing Papers

Make decorated place cards, notepapers, or greeting cards with pressed flowers. First, press your flowers between sheets of blotting paper weighted down with heavy books. Allow the flowers to dry, then glue them to fancy notepaper available from stationery stores. For an added touch, use a felt-tipped calligraphy pen to write your message.

> **The way to love anything is to realize that it might be lost.**
> **—G.K. Chesterton**

Tussie Mussie

There are many definitions suggested for the origin of the name "tussie mussie." The one I've always enjoyed is "to tickle the nose."

In Victorian times, certain flowers and herbs were designated as having specific meanings, such as "rosemary for remembrance." Thus, depending on the plant material in your bouquet, the medium became the message. A tussie mussie could say, "I love you" or perhaps "I do not like you at all!"

Supplies you will need:
Choose one small flower or rose for the center of your bouquet. Remember, your whole bouquet should fit in an aspirin or pill bottle. Gather any small fragrant herbs, such as rose geranium leaves, lamb's ears, or basil. Cut all stems to about 4 inches long on the diagonal and place in a glass of water for several hours. To start your bouquet, begin with your flower. Surround your flower with a small circle of one of the herbs. Add another circle of a different herb. Use floral tape or a pipe cleaner to hold stems together. Continue until you have a small bouquet, always keeping in mind the size of your container.

Take a 4-inch doily, fold it in half and make a small cut at the center of folded side. Unfold doily and refold in half again, in the opposite direction. The cut you made first will now be parallel to the folded edge. Make a cut at center as before. Unfold doily; there will be a small X cut in center of doily. Dry off any moisture around the stems and slip them through the doily. Press doily close around stems and secure with cellophane tape, floral pins, or floral tape. Now tie ribbons underneath doily. You may tie "love knots" in ribbon streamers. Now carefully set "tussie mussie" in its small container (labels removed of course). Be careful to only add enough water to cover bottom of stems, but not so much that doily becomes wet. Take your tussie mussie to a sick friend or one who needs cheering up. If you use fragrant herbs and flowers, the bouquet will smell wonderful. Depending on the plant material, it will probably dry well.

RAINY DAY CUPBOARD

Keep certain games and projects special by saving them especially for rainy days. Fill your "Rainy Day Cupboard" with all the ingredients to keep your kids busy, happy, and creative.

- Crayons, paints, markers, and colored pencils
- Construction paper
- Blank sketch books
- Pipe cleaners
- String
- Cardboard
- Wooden sticks from frozen treats
- Egg cartons
- Glue stick, white glue, and tape
- Glitter
- Scraps of fabric, lace, ribbons, and felt
- Stapler
- Stickers
- Scissors, pinking shears, safety scissors
- Magazines and used cards for cut-outs
- Wallpaper books

Memories & Special Occasions

Family Tree

A family reunion is the perfect time to display your family tree. If you've saved photographs through the years, you may be able to put one together for your family.

18" lengths of thick paper-covered wire for branches
photocopies of family photos
6" square of 1½"-thick green florist's foam
sheet moss
narrow ribbon or cord
craft glue

Use the paper-covered wire to make the branches. The number of branches you'll need on your tree depends on how many family members there are. Once the branches are counted, double the number. For example, if you have 4 children and 10 grandchildren, you would have 14 descendants and would need 28 pieces of paper-covered wire. Begin by grouping all the pieces of wire together. Two inches from the bottom, twist the wire together until it forms a 6-inch "trunk." Spread out the 2-inch bottom pieces…these will form the "roots" of the tree. At the top of your tree, divide the branches into groups of families, depending on how many people are in each family. Twist each group of wires together to make branches, leaving the strands fanned out at the ends to hold your pictures. For the base, cover the florist's foam with sheet moss. Place the roots of your tree into the foam for support. Punch a hole at the top of each photo. Attach a loop of ribbon or cord to each photo and tie to branches of the tree by family grouping.

Family Photo Calendar

Select 12 family photos. Photos of festive occasions, such as anniversaries, birthdays, and weddings, work very well. Make a color photocopy of each photo, enlarged to the size of the calendar page. Carefully glue one onto each month. A great gift!

Grandparent's Brag Book

Make a scrapbook just for grandparents who love to show off their grandchildren's latest accomplishments. Fill it with photos, awards, hand-drawn pictures, and a personal note from the grandchild. It's easy…use a small photo album with lots of pages. Tuck in all of your special items and you have an instant brag book. Let the grandchildren decorate the cover with their artwork.

Homemade Invitations

Make your own Tex-Mex party invitations. Purchase blank notes and envelopes and cut them into simple Western shapes like hats, boots, horses, cows, or cacti. Use corks to decorate your invitations. Draw a pattern on the wide end of a cork…a star, heart, chili pepper, or boot. Using a sharp knife, cut away the cork from the area outside the pattern, paring about 1/4" deep. Press the cork onto a stamp pad and press the design onto your invitations and envelopes. Use markers and gold glitter ("gold dust") to finish your designs.

Party Piñata

Kids love to take a whack at a real piñata…a papier-mâché donkey that's long been a Mexican party tradition. Remember to start early, as the papier-mâché will take several days to dry.

1/3 c. flour
1/4 c. water
plastic bag
large bowl
balloon
newspaper strips
egg carton
tape
4 empty bathroom tissue tubes
brightly colored poster paint

Mix flour and water and place in a plastic bag. Knead until it forms a paste. Put the paste in a large bowl and set aside. Blow up a balloon. Dip the newspaper strips into the paste and cover the balloon to make the body. While that is drying, roll newspaper into a tight ball to make the head and tape it to the balloon. Cover the head with newspaper dipped in paste. To make legs, wrap the cardboard bathroom tissue tubes in newspaper dipped in paste and tape to the body. Let the donkey dry for two days. Using brightly colored poster paints, add a mouth and eyes. Paint the body in any combination of colors and designs. Once the paint has dried, gently cut a hand-sized hole in the top of the body and fill with candy, gum, toys, and trinkets. Hang the piñata from a tree branch with string or twine. Let the kids take turns hitting the piñata with a large stick or baseball bat until it breaks, releasing the toys.

chapter five Country Kitchen

Soups & Starters

Fried Green Tomatoes

1 green tomato, sliced
1 egg, beaten
¼ c. seasoned Italian bread crumbs
2 T. Parmesan cheese
1 T. olive oil
slice of fresh lemon (optional)

Dip tomato slices into egg, then dredge in mixture of bread crumbs and cheese. In nonstick skillet, sauté in oil over medium heat, turning until slices are tender and both sides are browned. Sprinkle with fresh lemon juice, if desired. Serves 1 or 2.

Try drying your leafy green herbs in the refrigerator to preserve flavor and color. Harvest as usual, rinse, and pat dry. Put the leaves and/or stems in a brown paper bag. They will dry in three or four weeks.

Strawberry Soup

2 c. fresh strawberries or 2 10-oz. pkgs. frozen
1½ c. water
¾ c. sugar
1 c. cranberry juice
8 oz. strawberry yogurt
mint leaves for garnish

Blend ½ cup water and berries (saving 9 whole berries for garnish) until smooth. Put in a large pan and add sugar, remaining water, and cranberry juice; bring to a boil. Cool and whisk in yogurt. Refrigerate until cold. Garnish with the whole strawberries and mint leaves. Makes 9 ½-cup servings.

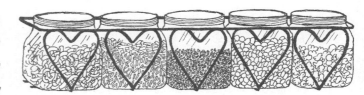

Cold Cucumber Soup

Take the heat out of summer with a bowl of this refreshing soup!

3 cucumbers, peeled, seeded, and cut into
   chunks
¼ t. salt
2 c. chicken broth
1 c. sour cream
3 T. fresh chives, minced
2 T. fresh dill, minced, for garnish

Combine cucumbers, salt, and one cup of the chicken broth in a blender or food processor. Cover; blend about one minute or until smooth. Transfer to a bowl and stir in the remaining chicken broth. Whisk in sour cream and herbs. Cover; chill. Garnish with fresh dill. Serves 6.

Zucchini Soup

Great served with French garlic bread!

12 to 16 oz. seasoned ground pork sausage
2 c. celery, cut into ½" pieces
1 c. onion, chopped
2 lb. zucchini, cut into ½" slices
14½ oz. can tomato sauce
2 green peppers, cut into ½" pieces
1 t. Italian seasoning
2 14½-oz. cans stewed tomatoes
½ t. basil
2 t. salt
1 T. sugar
½ to 1 c. water
¼ t. garlic powder
1 t. oregano
pepper to taste
Parmesan cheese for garnish

Brown sausage, drain off fat. Add celery and cook for 10 minutes, stirring occasionally. Add rest of ingredients, bring to a boil; cover pan, reduce heat, and simmer for 20 to 30 minutes. Ladle into bowls and top with Parmesan cheese. Serves 6 to 8.

Farmer's Market Soup

Dip your spoon to the bottom of a bowl of this soup and you will find the wonderful flavor of garlic and basil. If someone in your family doesn't like garlic, it's almost as good without the "buried treasure." Start with Step 1 the day before you plan to serve the soup.

Step 1: Mix the following ingredients and refrigerate in a covered bowl overnight.
28 oz. can crushed tomatoes
2 (or more) large cloves garlic
1½ T. dry basil

Step 2: Sauté these vegetables until tender.
2 T. vegetable oil
4 carrots, sliced thin
2 onions, chopped
3 stalks celery, sliced thin
1 small yellow turnip, cubed

Step 3: Add the following to the sautéed vegetables.
3 small zucchinis, sliced
19 oz. can cannellini (white kidney) beans
3 small summer squash, sliced
4 or 5 medium ripe tomatoes, peeled and cubed
water to cover and make soupy
salt as desired

Step 4: Add the following to the cooked vegetable mixture.
¼ to ⅓ lb. spaghetti, boiled until tender and drained. (Break the spaghetti before cooking if desired.)

To serve: Put 2 tablespoons of the cold tomato-garlic mixture in the bottom of a soup bowl. Add hot soup. Sprinkle with grated parmesan cheese (if desired) and serve.

Tomato Bruschetta

Add thin slices of Vidalia or purple sweet onion before grilling.

12 oz. loaf Italian bread cut in 1" diagonal slices
½ pint cherry tomatoes, cut into fourths
1 small yellow pepper, chopped
3 T. olive oil
3 cloves garlic (1 minced, 2 split in half)
1 T. fresh basil, chopped
2 T. Parmesan cheese, freshly grated

Place bread directly on grill (or on broiler rack in oven); lightly toast both sides about 2 minutes. In small bowl combine tomatoes, pepper, 1 tablespoon olive oil, minced garlic, and basil. Rub each toasted bread slice with split garlic cloves and then brush with olive oil. Spoon heaping spoonfuls of tomato mixture onto each slice and sprinkle with cheese. Makes 8 servings.

Stuffed Baked Brie

Garnish with grapes, fresh apple slices, and star fruit and serve crackers or crusty French bread alongside.

2 T. butter
4 large mushrooms, sliced
10" × 9" sheet frozen puff pastry, thawed
2 4-oz. pkgs. garlic and herb semi-soft cheese
14 oz. wheel Brie cheese
1 egg, beaten
1 T. water

In a skillet, melt butter over high heat. When butter begins to brown, add mushrooms and toss to coat. Sauté, stirring occasionally, until the mushrooms have browned around the edges, 2 to 3 minutes. Transfer the mushrooms to a plate. Lightly flour baking sheet. Place puff pastry on prepared sheet and roll out gently to remove fold lines. Spoon mushrooms in center of pastry. Spread one package semi-soft cheese on Brie and set on top of mushrooms (semi-soft cheese side down). Spread remaining semi-soft cheese on second side of Brie. Bring pastry up around sides and over cheese, wrapping completely and trimming excess pastry. Turn over and place seam side down. Gather pastry scraps and, using cookie cutters, cut out shapes of leaves (stars, hearts…your choice!) to place on top of pastry. (This recipe can be prepared one day ahead. Cover and refrigerate, but be sure to bring to room temperature before baking.) Combine egg and water. Brush over top. Preheat oven to 375°. Bake pastry until golden brown, 30 to 35 minutes. Let stand 10 minutes. Serve warm. Serves 8 to 10.

Chunky Gazpacho

Fresh tomatoes from the garden make this gazpacho very special. Serve in big, icy mugs garnished with stalks of celery.

2½ c. tomato juice
3 T. lemon juice
¼ c. plus 1 T. olive oil
6 large tomatoes, peeled and chopped
2 cucumbers, peeled, seeded, and chopped
½ c. green peppers, chopped
½ c. onion, finely chopped
1 clove garlic, minced
hot pepper sauce to taste
salt and pepper to taste

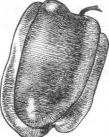

Whisk together tomato juice, lemon juice, and olive oil; set aside. In large mixing bowl, combine the chopped vegetables, and garlic; pour dressing over vegetables and mix. Add hot pepper sauce, salt, and pepper to taste. Cover and chill. Serve cold.

Tortilla Roll-Ups

Have an extra stack of tortillas ready for make-your-own roll-ups.

**8 oz. pkg. cream cheese, softened
4 oz. can green chilies, chopped
1 tomato, finely chopped
5 green onions, thinly sliced
2 oz. can black olives, sliced
5 soft flour tortillas**

Stir together cream cheese, chilies, tomato, onions, and olives, mixing well. Spread tortillas with cream cheese mixture and roll tightly. Chill tortillas for 2 to 3 hours and serve with salsa.

> If you ever find yourself with an overabundance of garlic, try this. Peel the cloves, cover with olive oil, and refrigerate in a tightly covered jar. The garlic lasts for months and the oil is great to cook with.

Pita Crisps

Easy to prepare ahead of time. Just store in an airtight container for snacking.

**3 T. virgin olive oil
½ t. sea salt (or coarse salt)
1 t. basil
12 oz. pkg. (about 5) large pita pockets cut into eighths**

Preheat oven to 450°. In mixing bowl, whisk together olive oil, salt, and basil. Add pita pieces and toss to coat well. Spread the pita triangles in a single layer onto cookie sheets and bake for 4 to 5 minutes, until crisp.

Nachos Magnifico

Vary the ingredients according to your creativity and taste.

vegetable cooking spray
1 lb. lean ground beef
1 c. onions, chopped
salt and pepper, to taste
2 15-oz. cans refried beans
4 oz. can green chilies, chopped
1 jar salsa
1 c. Cheddar cheese, shredded
1 c. mozzarella cheese, shredded
1 c. Monterey Jack cheese, shredded
6 oz. container guacamole
2¼ oz. can black olives, drained and sliced
1 c. green onion, chopped
1½ c. sour cream
tortilla chips

Preheat oven to 400°. Lightly grease 13" x 9" baking dish with cooking spray. In skillet, brown ground beef and onions; drain. Season with salt and pepper. Spread refried beans into bottom of baking dish and cover with beef. Layer on chilies and salsa. Sprinkle top with cheeses; cover and bake for 35 to 40 minutes. Top with guacamole, olives, onion, and sour cream. Serve right away with warm, crisp tortilla chips.

Stuffed Tulips

These stuffed tulips make a beautiful addition to a special Easter or spring buffet table.

6 tulip blossoms
6 eggs
¼ t. salt
4 T. sour cream
2 T. fresh chives, chopped
1 T. fresh dill, chopped
1 T. fresh tarragon, chopped

Remove the inside stem and gently wash and pat dry tulips. Boil eggs for 12 minutes, then cool quickly in cold water. Shell eggs and chop fine. Add salt, sour cream, chives, dill, and tarragon. Mix well. Fill tulip blossoms with the egg salad. The tulips may be eaten.

In recipes calling for fresh flowers, substitute half the amount if using dried. To dry flowers, gather early in the day, before the sun shines on them. Hang by the stems in a warm, dark area with good air circulation. Individual flowers can be dried differently. Place the clean flowers in a single layer on fine mesh. Let them dry in a warm, dark, dust-free area. Once flowers are dry, store them whole, crumbled, or pulverized in airtight glass containers in a cool, dark place.

Salads

Mandarin Orange, Spinach, & Almond Salad

A colorful spring salad, crunchy and different!

10 oz. bag fresh spinach, washed and drained
11 oz. can mandarin oranges, 2 T. juice reserved
½ c. extra virgin olive oil
3 T. balsamic vinegar
¼ c. honey-roasted almond slivers

In a salad bowl, combine spinach and mandarin oranges. In another bowl, whisk together mandarin orange juice, olive oil, and vinegar. Pour the dressing over the spinach and oranges and toss gently. Top with almonds.

> **Cherish all your happy moments;
> they make a fine cushion for old age.**
> **—Christopher Morley**

Curried Chicken Salad

The pineapple and curry add that gourmet touch.

2 c. cooked boneless chicken breasts, diced
1 apple, peeled and cubed
1 c. fresh pineapple, diced
¼ c. golden raisins
⅓ c. dates, chopped
2 T. chutney
½ t. salt

Dressing:
2 t. curry powder
1 c. mayonnaise
2 T. chicken broth

Combine salad ingredients together and refrigerate. While chilling, prepare dressing as follows: simmer curry and broth together for about 2 minutes, stirring constantly until it forms a smooth paste; cool and add paste to mayonnaise. One hour before serving, mix dressing with salad to allow flavors to blend, and return to refrigerator.

Rainbow Rotini Pasta Salad

For those who enjoy the taste of garlic, put a couple of cloves in the dressing and let sit for an hour or so. Then remove the cloves and pour over the salad.

1 or 2 boxes of tricolored rotini pasta
　　red/green/yellow peppers (use a variety
　　for color)
tomatoes
carrots
cucumbers
broccoli
onions (yellow, or use
　　Bermuda onions
　　for color)
cheese (your
　　favorite kinds,
　　chunked or
　　shredded)
Italian dressing

Cook pasta, drain, and let cool. The amount of vegetables you use depends on your taste. (Use lots of your favorites…or whatever is fresh and in season.) Add cut-up vegetables to the pasta. Mix Italian dressing with the above and stir until evenly coated. One large bottle is usually enough depending on your taste. For best results, let pasta sit overnight, and add more dressing if needed before serving. Try new pasta salads as "light" main meals. Finish with tastes of special cheeses and breads and complement with your favorite glass of wine or sparkling water.

Grilled Chicken Garden Salad

Especially delicious in the summer. Garnish with homemade star and heart croutons!

4 boneless, skinless chicken breasts
fat-free Italian dressing
4 slices of bread or one small French bread loaf
seasoned salt or butter-flavored sprinkles
1 head lettuce, leaf or romaine, torn
1 medium red onion, sliced and ringed
2 carrots, sliced or shredded
1 medium red or green pepper, sliced
2 tomatoes, chunked
12 oz. low-fat Parmesan or mozzarella cheese

Marinate chicken in Italian dressing for one hour in refrigerator. Grill marinated chicken until well done. When done, cut into strips or chunks. Cube bread, or use mini cookie cutters (stars, hearts) to cut bread. Toast on griddle with no-stick spray or butter. Sprinkle with seasoned salt or butter sprinkles. Keep turning. Prepare 4 plates with lettuce on each. Arrange onions, carrots, peppers, and tomatoes on lettuce. Sprinkle with cheese and Italian dressing. Place chicken and homemade croutons on top. Eat while chicken is hot or cold.

Surround a candle with a bed of parsley, radish roses, cauliflower, carrots, cucumbers, and celery sticks. This makes a colorful and edible centerpiece for a luncheon or casual meal.

Grilled Vegetable Salad

⅓ c. white balsamic vinegar
2 T. olive oil
2 shallots, finely chopped
1 t. dried Italian seasoning
¼ t. salt
¼ t. pepper
1½ t. molasses

Vegetables:
½ lb. carrots, scraped
1 red pepper
1 yellow pepper
2 yellow squash
1 large onion
2 zucchinis

Combine first seven ingredients in bowl. Set aside. Cut vegetables into large pieces and add to vinegar mixture, tossing to coat. Let stand 30 minutes, stirring occasionally. Drain, reserve vinegar mixture. Arrange vegetables in a grill basket that has been coated with cooking spray. Cook, covered with grill lid over medium to hot coals, 15 to 20 minutes, turning occasionally. Return vegetables to reserved vinegar mixture, tossing gently. Cover and refrigerate overnight. Yields 6 cups.

Wealth I ask not, hope nor love,
Nor a friend to know me;
All I ask, the heaven above
And the road below me.
—Robert Louis Stevenson

Black Bean & Salsa Salad

12 oz. can corn, drained
15 oz. can black beans, rinsed and drained*
1½ c. celery, chopped
½ c. green onion, chopped
¼ c. cilantro, chopped
14 oz. can salsa
¼ c. red wine vinegar dressing

In a large bowl combine corn, beans, celery, onion, and cilantro; mix well. Blend the salsa with the red wine vinegar dressing, pour over salad, and toss well. Cover and chill. Serves 8.

*You can also use navy, pinto, or kidney beans.

Pasta Salad

Good served with deviled eggs or French bread.

8 oz. pasta shells
½ c. green onions, sliced
½ c. fresh parsley, chopped
1 c. celery, sliced
1 c. frozen peas
1 c. fresh tomato, diced
1 c. ripe olives, sliced
½ c. mayonnaise
2 T. soy sauce (optional)
2 T. lemon juice
2 T. red wine vinegar
1 t. Dijon mustard
1 t. sugar
½ t. garlic powder
½ t. paprika
½ t. ground ginger
⅛ t. red hot pepper sauce
⅛ t. ground black pepper
3 c. cooked chicken, sliced (or 2 c. cooked shrimp)

Cook pasta according to directions on package until just tender (don't overcook). Rinse with cold water and drain. Place in a large bowl; add onion, parsley, celery, peas, tomatoes and olives. Combine mayonnaise with soy sauce (optional), lemon juice, vinegar, mustard, sugar, garlic powder, paprika, ginger, pepper sauce, and black pepper. Add to pasta mixture along with chicken or shrimp; mix well. (Adjust seasonings to your taste.) Chill overnight. To serve, pile into serving bowl or onto platter and garnish with tomato wedges, parsley, or lettuce. Makes 6 generous servings.

New Potato Salad

2 lb. new potatoes
½ c. celery, diced
3 hard-cooked eggs, sliced
8 oz. carton sour cream
1 T. fresh dill weed, chopped or 1 t. dried whole dill weed
2 T. vinegar
1 t. sugar
2 t. prepared horseradish
½ t. salt
½ t. dry mustard
⅛ t. pepper, freshly ground

Cook potatoes in boiling water, covered, for 20 minutes or until tender. Drain well and let cool. Peel potatoes, and slice into ½" slices. Combine potatoes, celery, and eggs in a large bowl and toss gently. Combine sour cream, dill weed, vinegar, sugar, horseradish, salt, dry mustard, and pepper in a small bowl. Pour over potato mixture and stir gently to coat. Chill thoroughly. Yields 6 to 8 servings.

Fresh Mozzarella & Tomato Salad

¼ c. olive oil
2 T. red wine vinegar
1½ t. fresh basil, chopped
¼ t. black pepper
¼ t. salt
2 to 3 large ripe tomatoes, sliced
8 oz. fresh mozzarella cheese, thinly sliced
red onions, sliced, for garnish

Mix together oil, vinegar, basil, pepper, and salt. Arrange tomato and cheese slices, alternately, on a large serving plate. Pour oil and vinegar dressing over tomatoes and cheese. Garnish with onions. Serve extra dressing with salad. Makes 4 servings.

Most of us agree, we can't improve on Mother Nature, so let's use fruits and vegetables as serving containers, instead of man-made ones. The garden outdoors suddenly grows indoors. Here are some suggestions:

- lemons and limes filled with ice-cream or sorbet
- cantaloupes filled with chicken or tuna salad
- red, yellow, and green peppers filled with dip
- tomatoes stuffed with shrimp salad
- oranges filled with marmalade or jam
- watermelon filled with fruit balls
- pumpkins and squash as soup tureens

Macaroni Salad

7 oz. elbow, shell or ring macaroni, uncooked
1 T. salt
10 oz. pkg. green peas, frozen
1 c. Cheddar cheese, cubed
1 c. sweet pickles, diced
¾ c. mayonnaise
½ c. onion, chopped
salt and pepper

Bring 3 quarts of water and 1 tablespoon salt to a rapid boil. Drop macaroni in and boil uncovered, stirring occasionally, just until tender (7 to 10 minutes). Drain immediately in colander and rinse with cold water. Cook peas as directed on package; drain. Mix macaroni, peas, cheese, sweet pickles, mayonnaise, and onion. Sprinkle with salt and pepper. Cover and refrigerate for at least 2 hours. Serves 6 to 8.

Antipasto Salad

Let your garden be your guide when making this antipasto salad. As summer moves on, use vegetables that are most plentiful. Enjoy!

1 sweet red pepper, cut into squares
1 c. cauliflower or broccoli
½ green pepper, cut into squares
½ c. yellow squash or zucchini
½ c. black olives, sliced
½ lb. pepperoni
½ lb. Swiss cheese, cubed in small
  squares
¼ c. Italian salad dressing

In a large bowl, combine all vegetables; add black olives, pepperoni, and cheese. Pour dressing on top; toss to coat. Cover and chill for at least 2 hours. Stir before serving. Serves 4.

> If you approach each new person you meet in a spirit of adventure, you will find yourself endlessly fascinated by the new channels of thought and experience and personality that you encounter. I do not mean simply the famous people of the world, but people from every walk of life.
> —Eleanor Roosevelt

Summer Garden Bean Salad

Adds zip to any summertime meal!

¾ c. sugar
⅓ c. vinegar
½ c. salad oil
salt and pepper to taste
1 lb. yellow beans, cooked and drained
1 lb. green beans, cooked and drained
1 lb. can red kidney beans, drained
1 green pepper, chopped
1 medium onion, sliced

Mix sugar, vinegar, oil, salt, and pepper until sugar is dissolved. Pour over beans, green pepper, and onion. Let refrigerate overnight.

Roasted Pepper Salad

6 red peppers, cut in half and seeded
3 stalks celery, in bite-size pieces
8 oz. jar small black olives, pitted
2 to 3 cloves garlic, minced
¼ c. olive oil
¼ c. white wine vinegar

Place pepper halves on a cookie sheet. Broil until the skins turn black and the peppers are scorched. Let cool in a paper bag for 15 to 20 minutes; peel the black part off the pepper to easily remove the skin. Cut the halves in long thin strips, and place in a bowl. Add celery, olives, garlic, olive oil, and vinegar.
Toss all ingredients together. Let marinate in the refrigerator. Makes 4 to 6 servings.

Greek Salad in a Pita Pocket

You can make a delicious sandwich out of most any vegetable salad with tasty pita bread.

fresh dill weed, chopped
½ t. dried oregano
1 sweet red bell pepper, sliced thin
1 t. garlic, crushed
¼ sweet red onion, sliced very thin
5 or 6 black Greek olives, pitted and sliced
½ ripe avocado, pitted and sliced
oil and vinegar salad dressing
4 large rounds of pita bread, sliced horizontally
    and halved
crumbled feta cheese to taste

Gently toss all salad ingredients in the dressing. Stuff into the pita pockets and enjoy! Serves 4.

Rosemary Chicken Salad

Can be prepared ahead of time and refrigerated until your luncheon.

3 c. cooked chicken breast, cubed
3 c. celery, thinly sliced
⅓ c. mayonnaise
⅓ c. sour cream
1 T. fresh rosemary, finely chopped

Combine chicken and celery. In a separate bowl, blend mayonnaise, sour cream, and rosemary. Combine chicken with dressing, and mix until well coated. Makes 4 servings.

Summer Vegetable Salad

A "just-right" medley of color, crunch, and spice!

1 c. fresh asparagus, blanched and chopped
1 c. fresh tomatoes, seeded and chopped
1 c. zucchini, shredded
1 c. red pepper, diced
2 t. balsamic vinegar
2 T. olive oil
7 dashes hot pepper sauce

Cook asparagus in small amount of boiling water until crisp-tender. In a salad bowl, combine tomato, zucchini, pepper, and asparagus. In another bowl, whisk together vinegar, oil, and hot pepper sauce. Combine dressing with salad just before serving.

There's no better way to flavor foods than with fresh herbs. Plant all your favorites for year-round use. Some favorites are coriander, parsley, chives, rosemary...

Blue Cheese Potato Salad

Try a variation of this recipe with baby red potatoes…no need to peel. Garnish with fresh dill.

8 c. potatoes, boiled, peeled, and cubed
½ c. scallions, chopped
½ c. celery, chopped
2 T. parsley, chopped
½ c. almond slivers, toasted
½ t. celery seed
2 t. salt
¼ t. pepper, freshly ground
½ c. blue cheese, crumbled
2 c. sour cream
¼ c. white wine vinegar
fresh dill, for garnish

In a large bowl, combine potatoes, scallions, celery, parsley, almonds, celery seed, salt, and pepper. In another bowl, mix together blue cheese, sour cream, and vinegar. Pour over potatoes and toss to coat. Chill overnight. Garnish with dill before serving.

Ginger~Lime Salad

The surprising taste of peaches makes this a very refreshing salad.

1 head green leaf lettuce, torn
1 ripe peach, pitted and thinly sliced
2 T. fresh parsley, torn
1½ T. fresh ginger, grated
3 T. lime juice
6 T. olive oil
1½ t. honey
salt and pepper to taste

In a large salad bowl, toss together lettuce, peaches, and parsley. In small mixing bowl, whisk ginger, lime juice, oil, and honey together and pour over salad. Season to taste with salt and pepper. Serve chilled.

Dips, Sauces, & Spreads

Spinach Dip

12 oz. container nonfat cottage cheese
10 oz. pkg. frozen chopped spinach, thawed
  and drained
1 T. lemon juice
1 c. nonfat mayonnaise
8 oz. can water chestnuts, drained and chopped
¼ c. dry vegetable soup mix
1 T. onion, grated

Blend cottage cheese in mixing bowl until smooth consistency. Place in medium-sized bowl. Add spinach and remaining ingredients to cottage cheese, stirring well. Serve with fresh vegetables or nonfat crackers. Makes about 3 cups.

Last night as I lay on the prairie,
And looked at the stars in the sky,
I wondered if ever a cowboy
Would drift to that sweet bye-and-bye.
—"The Cowboy's Dream"

Barbecue Sauce

Use as marinade or basting sauce for meat.

½ c. low-calorie catsup
2 c. diet cola

Combine beverage and catsup until well blended. Store in airtight container in refrigerator.

Chili Con Queso Dip

Serve with tortilla chips, crisp cold veggies, and baked pita slices.

28 oz. can plum tomatoes, drained and chopped
2 4-oz. cans green chilies, drained and seeded
1 c. heavy cream
1 lb. Cheddar cheese, shredded
salt and pepper to taste

Over low heat, cook the tomatoes and chilies for about 15 minutes. Stirring constantly, add cream and cheese and continue cooking until mixture thickens. Season with salt and pepper and serve warm.

Peach Jam

So easy to make, so rich and tangy. Keeps in the refrigerator for weeks.

1 lb. dried peaches
½ to ¾ c. sugar
3 to 4 T. cognac

In heavy saucepan, cover peaches with water and simmer until it becomes a jamlike consistency. Stir in sugar and cognac to taste. Continue cooking over low heat until sugar is thoroughly dissolved and jam is thick. Let cool and refrigerate.

HERB & SPICE BUTTER LOGS

Try combining softened sweet butter with herbs and spices. Then roll into logs with waxed paper and refrigerate until hard. Delicious on fresh breads, sweet corn, broiled salmon, and potatoes. Experiment with different combinations...dill with lemon and paprika; rosemary with mint; chives with freshly ground pepper; tarragon with lemon; basil with garlic, oregano, and pine nuts. Just slice off the butter in rounds to serve. Remember, a little goes a long way!

Pear Chutney

Gourmet preserves make beautiful holiday gifts.

5 pears, peeled, seeded, and chopped
3 apples, peeled, seeded, and chopped
3 peaches, peeled, pitted, and chopped
2 lemons, seeded and chopped
2 tomatoes, peeled and chopped
1 lime, seeded and chopped
3½ t. dried red pepper, crushed
3 c. brown sugar, packed
1½ c. raisins
1 t. cinnamon
1 t. cloves
¼ t. nutmeg
½ c. crystallized ginger

In large pot, combine all ingredients and simmer for 2½ hours. Pack into sterilized jars.

Dilly Shrimp Dip

Great for a summer dinner party!

8 oz. pkg. cream cheese,
    softened
8 oz. shrimp, cleaned
    and chopped
1 c. celery, chopped
2 T. sour cream
1 T. mayonnaise
1 T. mustard
1 T. ketchup
1 T. onion, chopped
½ t. dill
1 t. parsley

Put all ingredients in your blender or food processor and blend until smooth. Chill and serve with crackers or bagel chips.

Hot Broccoli Dip

This recipe works equally well with fresh or frozen broccoli. It is an excellent topping for new red potatoes, which are both ready about the same time in my garden. We also like it as a topping for baked potatoes in the winter and as a hot dip for tortilla chips any time of the year. Your kids just might LOVE broccoli if you try this recipe.

1 lb. fresh broccoli or 16 oz. pkg. frozen, cooked,
    drained and chopped into bite-size pieces
16 oz. pasteurized processed cheese spread
2 4-oz. cans sliced mushrooms, drained
10¾ oz. can cream of mushroom soup
10¾ oz. can cream of onion soup

Melt cheese in microwave. Stir all ingredients together into a crock pot. Cook until hot and well blended.

HERB-INFUSED VINEGARS

A tall, pretty glass bottle of vinegar makes a lovely gift when a few leaves or stalks of freshly picked herbs are added. Choose white cider or wine vinegar. Add tarragon and chives, rosemary and garlic, lavender, orange, and mint or basil and oregano. Experiment to find just the right combination for salads and marinades.

10-Layer Mexicale Dip

This is excellent with fresh garden tomatoes, green peppers, etc. Only make a few hours before or it can get runny. I cut up veggies ahead and place in baggies, then when I want to make it, I just start layering. You will find that on a day when it is too hot to cook or no one feels like eating much, this is great. Just put it out on the porch along with a basket of tortilla chips, and some cool drinks, and watch it disappear! They will clean it up and look for more. Serves 6 to 8.

16 oz. can refried beans
1 pt. sour cream, divided
large green pepper
12 oz. jar salsa
8 to 12 oz. sharp Cheddar cheese, shredded
large tomato, diced
medium onion (red or yellow), diced
8 to 12 oz. mozzarella cheese, shredded or
**   prepackaged taco cheese**

Using a fork, spread refried beans on the bottom of a 9" x 9" pan (or double the recipe and use a 13" x 9" pan). Stir ½ pint of sour cream until pourable; spread over beans. Cut green pepper into thin slivers, and place half of them over sour cream. Put salsa (mild, medium or hot, your choice) in a strainer for a few minutes to drain a bit, and then pour over pepper slices. Spread cheddar cheese evenly over salsa. Stir the other ½ pint of sour cream until pourable, spread over cheese. Add diced tomato (if it is really juicy, put in a strainer for a few minutes). Next add the rest of the green pepper slivers. Place the diced onion on top of the pepper slices. Top with mozzarella cheese (or a prepackaged taco cheese).

Guacamole

2 c. (2 large) avocados, mashed
2 T. lemon juice or 1 T. lemon juice
**   and 1 T. lime juice**
tomato, diced (optional)
green chilies, finely chopped
¼ t. salt
¼ t. chili powder
1 T. onion, grated or finely chopped
⅛ t. garlic powder

Combine all ingredients. Chill and serve.

Breads & Muffins

Blueberry Whole Wheat Yogurt Muffins

This is my most-requested recipe. It is a favorite at my office, where they don't even know it is a low-fat recipe.

1 c. all-purpose flour
1 c. whole wheat flour
⅓ c. plus 1 T. sugar
¼ t. salt
2 t. baking soda
¼ c. unsweetened orange juice
8 oz. carton of vanilla low-fat yogurt
2 T. vegetable oil
1 t. vanilla extract
1 egg
1 c. fresh or frozen blueberries, thawed

Preheat oven to 400°. Spray 12 muffin cups with cooking spray. Combine the first 5 ingredients in a large bowl. (Do not pack flour into measuring cups! Stir it in its storage container and then scoop it into a measuring cup, leveling off with a flat spatula.)

Make a well in the center of the dry ingredient mixture. Combine orange juice and the next four ingredients in a separate bowl; stir well. Add to dry ingredients, stirring until just moistened. Gently fold in blueberries. Spoon batter into muffin cups, filling almost to the top. Sprinkle one tablespoon of sugar evenly onto muffins. Bake for 18 minutes or until golden. Remove from pans immediately. Cool on wire rack. Yields 11 to 12 muffins.

Lemon–Butter Muffins

Luscious served with our peach jam.

½ c. fresh lemon juice
2 large eggs
2 T. lemon rind, freshly grated
½ c. butter, melted
2 c. all-purpose flour, unsifted
½ c. plus 2 T. sugar
1 T. baking powder
1 t. salt

Preheat oven to 400°. Grease 2 muffin tins well. Stir lemon juice, eggs, and lemon rind into melted butter. In another bowl, mix together flour, ½ cup sugar, baking powder, and salt; make a well in the center. Stir in egg mixture and blend until well moistened. Pour into muffin tins, filling each cup about two-thirds full. Sprinkle tops of muffins with remaining 2 tablespoons of sugar. Bake for 15 to 20 minutes or until lightly browned. Makes 18 to 24 muffins.

Oatmeal Bread

3 c. oatmeal
1 T. salt
⅓ c. plus 2 T. honey
1¾ c. heavy cream
¼ c. butter
⅓ c. lukewarm water
2 T. yeast
2 c. unbleached white flour

Grease 3 bread pans. Preheat oven to 375°. Combine oatmeal, salt, and ⅓ cup honey in a large bowl. In a saucepan, heat cream, butter, and water until butter is melted. Pour butter mixture over the oatmeal mixture and allow to stand until just lukewarm. In a separate bowl, combine the warm water, yeast, and 2 tablespoons honey and allow to sit while oatmeal is cooling. When yeast is bubbling, combine the yeast-honey mixture with the oatmeal mixture and gradually add flour until dough is stiff. Knead for about 5 minutes on a floured breadboard, until dough is smooth. Grease a bowl and place dough in it to rise for about an hour, or until it has doubled. Punch down the dough and separate it into 3 medium-sized loaves. Place into greased bread pans and let rise again for about 45 minutes. Bake for 40 to 45 minutes, or until the crust sounds hollow when thumped with your finger.

Honey Wheat Germ Bread

More than anything, it's the old-fashioned taste of home.

2 pkgs. dry yeast
1 c. warm water
4 c. white flour
2 T. brown sugar
2 t. salt
¼ c. honey
1¾ c. milk, scalded and cooled slightly
1¾ c. whole wheat flour
¼ c. wheat germ

Grease 2 standard loaf pans. Preheat oven to 375°. In large mixing bowl combine yeast, water, ½ cup of white flour, brown sugar, and salt; beat until smooth. Let stand covered in warm place for 15 minutes. Add honey, milk, wheat flour, and wheat germ. Beat 2 minutes with mixer and gradually add white flour. Fold out onto floured surface and shape into smooth ball. Cover with mixing bowl and let stand 10 minutes. Knead thoroughly and divide into 2 balls. Cover and let rest again. Shape each ball into a loaf and place in pans. In warm place, cover and let rise until doubled.
Bake for 35 to 40 minutes.

Croutons

Be frugal and make your own croutons using your stale bread and rolls! Cut bread in small pieces and place in a large mixing bowl. Melt butter or margarine and add herbs (oregano, onion, garlic, or whatever herb you choose). Pour over bread cubes, stir, and spread on a cookie sheet. Preheat oven to 300°. Bake 15 minutes, turn, then bake 15 minutes more. I make large batches and store in the freezer. For a variety, try a mixture of cinnamon and sugar or Parmesan cheese instead of herbs. Herbed croutons are delicious on those fresh garden salads of lettuce, tomatoes, cukes, and peppers.

Turn the porch into a room that says "summer." Paint the floor white. If you have wicker or metal furniture, give it a fresh coat of white paint. Cover the cushions in fresh blue-and-white checks or stripes. Add a natural sisal mat or blue-and-white rag rug. If you have space, fill a windowbox with the colors of fresh plants in terra-cotta pots...green ivies, yellow sunflowers, red geraniums.

Annie's No-Knead French Bread

My friend always adds parsley, sage, rosemary, and thyme...and, of course, we just had to name it "Simon and Garfunkel Bread" from the lyrics of the song. It is bound to become a family favorite!! I often like to make round loaves (I think they are more attractive) by placing the dough in well-buttered ovenware dishes (about 3" deep and approximately 6" in diameter).

1 pkg. yeast
1 T. sugar
2 c. lukewarm water
1 t. salt
4 c. white flour
herbs (optional)

Dissolve yeast and sugar in lukewarm water. Add other ingredients and beat well. Dough will be soft and sticky. Allow dough to rise in mixing bowl until it doubles in bulk. Stir down, divide dough evenly into two loaf pans, and let rise again. Place in cold oven. Turn heat to 400° and bake for 30 minutes. Bread is done when it is brown on top and, when thumped, gives a hollow sound. If you want an herb bread (and who doesn't?), add herbs as you stir down the dough just before putting into pans. Hint: one tablespoon of herbs usually makes a mildly flavored loaf...add more if desired, to suit taste.

The more passions and desires one has, the more ways one has of being happy.
— Charlotte-Catherine

Potted Herb Bread

Makes a terrific and unusual bread and floral presentation for entertaining.

2 pkg. yeast
1 c. warm water
1 c. milk
⅓ c. sugar
1 t. salt
3 eggs
½ c. butter
3 T. favorite herbs
3 to 4 c. flour

Sprinkle yeast over water in a small bowl. Stir to dissolve. Heat together milk, sugar, and salt until slightly warm. Beat eggs; add yeast, milk mixture, and butter. Add herbs (rosemary, garlic powder, oregano, thyme, whatever you like. If you wish to use sage, use only half the amount). Add enough flour to make soft dough. Knead lightly and place in lightly greased bowl in a warm, draft-free spot, cover and let rise until dough doubles in bulk (approximately 1 hour). In the meantime, grease well 6 small (5") flowerpots and flour generously. Punch down dough and shape the dough into a long roll. More herbs may be added to jelly roll style—roll, if desired. Cut into six 3" rolled pieces. Shape in flowerpots (filling pots three-quarters full) and place pots onto cookie sheet. Let rise again (approximately 1 more hour). Bake at 350° for 12 to 18 minutes or until golden brown. For the last 5 minutes brush with beaten egg. Sprinkle top with a mixture of dried herbs, fresh cracked pepper and salt. Note: Bread may be difficult to remove from flowerpots if the pots are not greased and floured enough.

Beverages

Creamy Kiwi Freeze

1 kiwi, peeled
½ c. vanilla nonfat frozen yogurt
2 T. honey
½ c. seltzer or club soda,
    chilled

About 5 minutes before
serving, cut kiwi in quarters.
In blender at high speed,
blend kiwi, frozen yogurt and
remaining ingredients 1 minute.
Pour into 2 chilled glasses.
Makes 2 servings.

**When serving friends
summer beverages, I sometimes float
various colors of pansies in their glasses.
It's easy to refill glasses when guests
remember the color of their flower (the
pansies are also safe to eat).**

Tropical Magic

1 small mango
8 oz. can pineapple
    chunks in
    unsweetened
    pineapple juice
1 c. seltzer or club
    soda, chilled
3 ice cubes
¼ t. coconut
    extract

About 10 min-
utes before
serving, peel
mango and
cut into bite-
size pieces. In
blender at high
speed, blend
mango, pineapple with
its juice, and remaining
ingredients for one minute. Pour into 2 chilled
glasses. Makes 2 servings.

Blushing Pink Punch Bowl

Float pink and white rose petals and slices of lime on top.

2 c. hibiscus tea leaves
2 qts. boiling water
1½ c. honey
2 qts. sparkling water
1 gallon rosé wine

Garnish:
1 lime, sliced
rose petals

Tie the loose tea into a cheesecloth bag and drop in boiling water. Steep, covered, about 10 minutes. Remove tea bag and add honey, stirring to dissolve. Cool completely and pour into a gallon container. Add sparkling water and stir. To serve, mix tea with wine in a punch bowl over ice and add rose petals and lime as garnish. Makes 2 gallons.

Minty Iced Tea

For best tea results, always bring fresh, cold water to a rolling boil.

8 c. boiling water
8 mint herbal tea bags
8 c. ice cubes
fresh mint sprigs, for garnish

In large glass container, pour water over tea bags and allow to steep for 30 minutes. Remove tea bags; stir in sugar and half of ice cubes. Pour into glasses full of ice and top each with a fresh sprig of mint. Serves 12.

Tennessee Fruit Tea

Especially refreshing after gardening!

4 to 5 T. unsweetened instant tea
4 c. water
1½ c. sugar
12 oz. can frozen lemonade
12 oz. can frozen pineapple orange juice

Stir together tea, water, and sugar; bring to a boil, then let cool. In a gallon container mix lemonade and pineapple orange juice. Add to the tea mixture along with enough water to make one gallon. Refrigerate. Serve over ice.

When you place your sun tea out in the morning, put a few sprigs of mint, lemon balm, scented geraniums, lemon verbena, or some rose petals in your jar. Strain out when you are ready to serve.

California Lemonade

Cardamom is a fragrant spice from India that tastes much like cinnamon.

1½ c. sugar
1 c. lemon juice, freshly squeezed
5 cardamom seeds, ground

Boil sugar and lemon juice at medium heat for 8 to 10 minutes. Remove from heat and cool. Add cardamom seeds and store in refrigerator. To prepare lemonade, mix one tablespoon of concentrate with one cup sparkling water.

Summer Slush

I remember having this slush in hot summer afternoons on my grandmother's back porch.

46 oz. can of pineapple juice
12 oz. can frozen orange juice
3 c. sugar
lemon-lime carbonated drink
46 oz. water

Combine all of the above ingredients in a saucepan and boil until sugar dissolves. Pour into a 13" × 9" pan and a loaf pan. Cover with foil and freeze until firm. To serve, cut out chunks with a knife, place in a glass, and pour your favorite lemon-lime carbonated beverage over it. Head for the shade of the back porch.

If you have an older home with a brand-new deck, you may want to give your deck a more weathered, aged appearance. It's easy! Just mix 1 cup baking soda with 1 gallon of water. Apply to deck and let it dry. Rinse off and apply a waterproof sealer. Your deck will look like it's been home to many summer gatherings.

Friendship Punch

3 T. dried rosemary or
  1½ T. fresh
1 c. water
6 oz. can frozen limeade
1 t. vanilla
12 oz. can apricot
  nectar
2 qt. ginger ale
Johnny jump-ups, violets,
  or rosemary flowers,
  for garnish

Simmer rosemary in water for 2 minutes. Cool completely and strain. Combine remaining ingredients (well chilled) and serve in a punch bowl decorated with an ice ring. Johnny jump-ups, violets, or rosemary flowers may be floated on punch for a special touch.

Old-Fashioned Lemonade

Nothing beats a glass of cold lemonade on a hot summer day!

4 lemons
¾ c. sugar
4 c. cold water

Cut lemons into thin slices, remove seeds. Place slices in a large nonmetal bowl; sprinkle with sugar and let stand for 10 minutes. Press lemons with the back of a spoon to extract juice. Add water, stirring and pressing lemons. Remove lemon slices and serve over ice. Garnish with additional lemon slices. Makes 4 servings.

TEA BASKET

If your mother is a tea drinker, fill a basket with some teatime favorites...a special mug or cup, flavored and herbal tea bags, a silver teaspoon, sugar cubes or packets, and even a tiny book about tea. A perfect gift for Mother's Day!

Summer Strawberry Cooler

4 c. fresh strawberries
1½ c. sugar
4⅔ orange juice
4 c. ice cubes
⅔ c. ginger ale

In a blender combine strawberries, sugar, and 1 cup of orange juice. Process until smooth. Pour mixture into pitcher. Slowly blend remaining orange juice with ice until mixture is slushy. Mix orange "slush" with berry mixture and ginger ale in large container. Serve. Makes approximately 4 quarts.

There are few hours in life more agreeable than the hours dedicated to the ceremony known as afternoon tea.
—Henry James

Rose Petal Tea

2 c. firmly packed fragrant rose petals
  (about 15 large roses, wash and pat dry)
1 c. tea leaves

Preheat oven to 200°. Place rose petals on an ungreased baking sheet. Leaving oven door slightly open, dry petals in oven for 3 to 4 hours or until completely dry, stirring occasionally. In a food processor, fitted with steel blade, process rose petals and tea leaves until finely chopped. Store in an airtight container.

To brew tea: Place 1 teaspoon tea for each 8 ounces of water in a warm teapot. Bring water to a rolling boil and pour over tea. Steep 5 minutes. Stir and strain. Serve hot or chilled. Serves 3.

Rose Petal Ice Cubes

These look so pretty floating in a bowl of punch or a pitcher of iced tea or lemonade. A perfect touch for an outdoor wedding, bridal shower, or garden tea party!

Collect pesticide-free rose petals. Rinse under warm water and blot dry. Fill ice cube tray half full with water and freeze. Place a rose petal on each cube, cover with a teaspoon of water; freeze again. Fill cubes completely with water and freeze, remove from trays.

Cookouts & Picnics

Smoked Salmon Cones with Horseradish Cream

These appetizers can be prepared ahead and refrigerated for up to 3 hours.

6 slices brown bread, crusts removed, thinly sliced
½ c. heavy cream
2 T. horseradish
10 oz. smoked salmon, very thinly sliced into 2" squares

Cut each bread slice into 4 squares. Wrap in plastic and set aside. Beat cream until smooth, and stiff peaks form; add horseradish. To assemble, roll salmon squares into cone shapes and place on bread squares. Using a pastry bag, fill each salmon cone with horseradish cream. Makes 24 cones.

If you want to encourage conversation, seat your guests at a round table, not too far apart.

Herb Burgers

These are moist, tender, and delicious! We serve these on the 4th of July with all the trimmings.

1 tomato, seeded and finely chopped
½ c. ripe olives, chopped
1 t. pressed garlic
⅓ c. green chillies, chopped
2 t. creamy mustard blend
1 t. fresh oregano, chopped
2 t. chili powder
1 t. fresh lemon thyme, chopped
1 T. fresh dill leaves, chopped
    or 1 t. dried
1 T. fresh parsley, chopped
2 T. fresh cilantro leaves, chopped
¼ c. onion, minced (I use vidalias)
2 t. fresh basil, chopped or ½ t. dried
2 t. fresh lemon zest, grated
1 lb. lean ground beef

Mix together all ingredients except the beef. Add beef and mix lightly (overmixing makes it more like meatloaf). Shape into 4 or 5 patties. Grill for 4 to 5 minutes on each side. Turn only once.

Cucumber Sandwiches Dijon

A traditional tea must include crisp cucumber sandwiches!

1 cucumber, peeled and thinly sliced
¼ t. salt
1 T. olive oil
1 T. fresh lemon juice
1 t. sugar
pepper to taste
¼ lb. butter, softened
½ t. Dijon mustard
1 T. lemon juice
20 slices good-quality white bread, crusts removed

Place the cucumber slices in a colander, sprinkle with salt and cover with a plate, weighing the plate down with a soup can to drain out the excess juice. Allow to sit for 1 or 2 hours, pressing the juice out occasionally. Combine oil, lemon juice, sugar, and pepper and combine with the cucumbers. In a separate bowl, cream butter, mustard, and lemon juice. Blend the butter and Dijon musturd. Spread the bread with the Dijon butter. Drain the cucumbers on paper towels and arrange on 10 slices of the bread, topping with the other 10 slices. Cut each sandwich into 4 triangles. Arrange on a platter garnished with fresh leaf lettuce.

Pinwheel Sandwiches

Cover these appetizers with moistened lettuce leaves to prevent them from drying out before serving.

6 slices soft white bread, thinly sliced
¾ c. sandwich filling

Roll out bread slices with a rolling pin until flat. Spread slices with your favorite filling (some of our favorites: crab salad with dill and tuna salad with rosemary.) Rolling the bread, spread side up, roll each slice into long rolls. When ready to serve, slice the rolls into ½" slices and arrange pinwheels on appetizer tray.

Salmon and Cream Cheese Sandwiches

For a colorful variation, add pimentos to this cream cheese mixture.

¼ lb. smoked salmon, thinly sliced
4 oz. cream cheese, softened
1 T. fresh dill, minced
8 slices pumpernickel bread, crusts removed
dill sprigs for garnish

Combine salmon, cream cheese, and dill. Spread salmon mixture over bread slices, and cut into fingers or squares. Garnish with tiny sprigs of fresh dill.

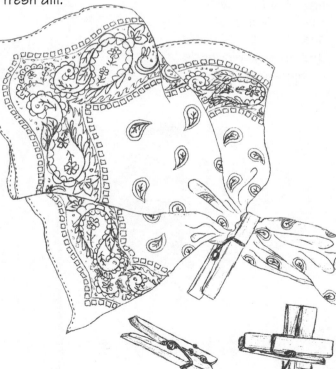

Lime and Ginger Grilled Salmon

Arrange slices of fresh lemon and lime alongside.

2 lbs. salmon fillet, skinned and boned
2 T. fresh ginger, minced
2 T. lime zest
½ t. salt
½ t. pepper, freshly ground
½ t. lime juice, freshly squeezed
2 T. butter, melted, or olive oil
lemon and lime slices for garnish

Heat grill. Sprinkle salmon with ginger, lime zest, salt, and pepper. In small bowl, combine lime juice and butter. Brush salmon with melted butter and grill about 5 minutes per side, or until done. Makes 4 servings.

Different-colored bandanas make colorful napkins for any barbecue. Tie one around each person's set of utensils. After the party, just toss them in the wash.

Grilled Garlic Burgers

Serve with a platter of fresh lettuce, slices of vine-ripened tomato, pickles, and onions for toppings.

1¾ lbs. lean ground beef
2 T. garlic, minced
½ c. onion, finely chopped
2 t. salt
2 t. pepper, freshly ground
6 oz. fresh horseradish, peeled and shredded
1 T. vegetable oil
2 T. mustard
½ c. plus 2 T. ketchup
2 T. sour cream
4 fresh onion buns

In a mixing bowl, mix ground beef, garlic, onion, salt, and pepper. Shape into 4 patties. Sprinkle with horseradish and press into meat. Coat grill or large skillet with oil and cook burgers for 4 to 5 minutes per side. While cooking, mix together mustard, ketchup, and sour cream. Top burgers with ketchup mixture and serve on grilled buns.

Beer Steamed Shrimp

Save your shrimp shells for up to three months in the freezer… they can be boiled to make a flavorful fish stock for chowder.

2 T. lemon juice
1 T. prepared seafood seasoning
1 can beer
1 lb. shrimp, peeled and deveined

In a large saucepan, combine lemon juice, seafood seasoning, and beer; bring to boil. Add shrimp; cover and steam for about 3 to 5 minutes until pink and tender. Drain. Serve hot or cold.

LIGHTING IDEAS

Lighting is extremely important to the atmosphere of any party. Most parties need two types of lighting…one to light the scenery and the other to add glow to tables and other eating areas. You can achieve a party mood with bamboo torches, paper lanterns, luminarias (votive candles nestled in sand inside open paper bags), strings of colored lights, or tiny white lights. For table lighting, use votive candles tucked inside colored beverage glasses, jelly jars, or little clay pots. Taper candles work well inside hurricane shades, and pillar candles can be placed inside crocks, buckets, or big clay pots. For even more sparkle, string tiny white lights along your buffet table.

Barbecued Baby Back Ribs

Boiling the ribs first tenderizes them and removes excess fat.

2 T. olive oil
1 onion, chopped
1 stalk celery, chopped
1 clove garlic, peeled and finely chopped
1 c. ketchup
¼ c. brown sugar, packed
¼ c. red wine vinegar
2 T. Worcestershire sauce
1 T. Dijon mustard
1½ lbs. baby back ribs

Heat oil in a saucepan, then add onion, celery, and garlic. Sauté about 5 minutes, until tender. Add all remaining sauce ingredients, stirring and simmering for about 10 minutes. Put sauce in food processor and whirl until smooth. Allow sauce to cool slightly. Bring a pot of water to a boil; simmer ribs, covered, for about 20 minutes. Drain ribs and dry with paper towels; baste generously with sauce. Grill for 5 to 6 minutes on one side. Turn ribs and baste again. Grill for 6 minutes longer and serve with extra sauce.

Cornmeal Fried Chicken

Orange flavors add a sunny taste to this savory, golden chicken!

3 T. orange zest
2 T. orange juice
1 c. milk
3 lbs. frying chicken or 8 chicken breasts
⅔ c. cornmeal
⅔ c. flour
1 t. salt
1 t. pepper, freshly ground
3½ c. sunflower or safflower oil

In a large bowl, combine orange zest, orange juice, and milk. Soak chicken in this mixture for half an hour. Meanwhile, in a brown paper bag, combine cornmeal, flour, salt, and pepper. Heat oil in a large skillet (filling about 2" deep) until it reaches 350°. Coat chicken pieces one at a time by shaking in bag of cornmeal mixture. Fry chicken in oil about 20 minutes, or until juices run clear when pricked with a fork (breasts cook more quickly). Drain on paper towels.

Coconut Shrimp

Garnish with fresh orange slices.

1½ c. oil
1 c. beer
1 c. flour
1 lb. shrimp, shelled and cleaned
14 oz. pkg. shredded coconut
orange slices, for garnish

Pour oil into large fryer and heat to 375°. Mix together flour and beer until it makes a batter. Coat shrimp in batter, then roll in coconut. Fry shrimp in small batches about 2 to 3 minutes until golden and curled. Drain on paper towels.

Mixed Green Slaw

A slaw without cabbage...cool, refreshing, and low-fat.

2 c. romaine lettuce, thinly sliced
2 c. watercress, stems removed
2 c. radicchio, thinly sliced
½ c. plain low-fat yogurt
2 T. fresh lime juice
1 T. olive oil
salt and pepper to taste
¼ c. green olives, pitted and chopped

Toss the greens together in a large salad bowl. In a separate bowl, whisk together the remaining ingredients. Toss the salad in the dressing just before serving. Serves 6.

Here's a tip for any buffet table... stack your plates at the beginning, but save the silverware, napkins, and beverages for the end of the table. So much easier to handle!

Ham & Pineapple Kabobs

The tropical flavor of Hawaii on a stick!

3 lbs. ready-to-eat ham, cut into 1" chunks
¼ c. soy sauce
¼ c. bourbon
¼ c. dark brown sugar
½ t. ground ginger
fresh pineapple, peeled and sliced in chunks
2 or 3 green peppers, cut into chunks
2 or 3 sweet onions, cut into chunks
1 lb. cherry tomatoes
wooden skewers

Marinate ham in mixture of soy sauce, bourbon, brown sugar, and ginger for at least 30 minutes. Reserving marinade, arrange ham, pineapple, peppers, onions, and tomatoes on skewers. (Don't forget to soak your skewers in water before using them.) Place on a hot grill and cook, brushing with marinade, about 3 minutes per side or until vegetables begin to brown.

CAMPFIRE TIPS

You don't have to be an expert to know how to build a campfire! Begin by clearing an area around the site. Gather some rocks to form a ring around the clearing, building up the sides to about 6 to 8 inches. Start with lighting "tinder," something that burns easily like small dry twigs, wood shavings, or crumpled paper. (If you have some old candle stubs, place them in the center; this assures your fire will catch.) Make a small pile of sticks stacked like a teepee loosely around the shavings or paper. Add larger sticks and then logs of hard wood as the fire matures. Keep feeding your fire every hour or so until you have deep, hot coals. To extinguish, smother the fire with "clean" dirt or sand (no leaves or sticks) and douse with water. Before leaving your campsite, make sure coals are completely extinguished and all litter is gathered.

To keep certain foods cold (like potato salad), freeze a stoneware bowl ahead of time. Just before leaving for your picnic, transfer food into the frozen bowl and cover with foil. This will keep the food cold for a longer period of time.

Grilled Strip Steaks with Herb~Mustard Sauce

Who can resist the aroma of steaks on the grill?

2 cloves garlic, crushed
2 t. water
2 T. Dijon mustard
1 t. basil
½ t. pepper
½ t. thyme
2 boneless strip or rib eye steaks, 2½ to 3" thick
salt to taste

On high power, microwave garlic and water together. Stir in mustard, basil, pepper, and thyme; spread onto both sides of steaks. Place steaks on grid over medium ash-covered coals and grill. Grill loin steaks 8 or 9 minutes per side, rib eye steaks 6 to 7 minutes per side (depending on thickness) for medium-rare to medium doneness. Season steaks with salt as desired. Carve steaks crosswise into thick slices. Makes 4 servings.

Pan~Fried Trout

If your celebration includes a fishing trip, fresh trout is the way to go!

½ c. cornmeal
½ c. flour
¾ T. salt
1 T. pepper
2 onions, thinly sliced
1 lb. bacon, fried (reserve some of grease)
1 to 2 fresh trout, cleaned

Mix together cornmeal, flour, salt, and pepper; set aside. In large frying pan, sauté onions in bacon grease. Dredge fish in cornmeal mixture and coat both sides well. Fry fish in hot grease and onions until very crisp. Garnish with crispy bacon.

Texas Border Barbecued Beef Ribs with Red-Hot Chili Sauce

Make the chili sauce the night before to allow the flavors to ripen. Serve extra sauce at the table.

Red-Hot Chili Sauce:
2 T. lard
2 T. flour
¼ c. mild red chili pepper, ground
2 c. beef bouillon
¼ t. cilantro, crushed
¼ t. ground cumin

Melt lard in a large saucepan over medium heat. Gradually add flour, stirring with a fork until flour turns golden brown. Remove pan from heat and stir in chili pepper, then bouillon. Return pan to heat and add remaining ingredients. Simmer, uncovered, 30 to 45 minutes. Adjust seasonings to taste. Allow to cool, then refrigerate overnight. Makes 2 cups.

Marinade:
⅓ c. red chili sauce (above recipe)
1 c. dry red wine
2 T. olive oil
1 large clove garlic, minced
1 small yellow onion, diced
½ t. salt
1 clove garlic, minced
¾ t. salt
freshly ground black pepper
    to taste
4 lbs. beef short ribs

Combine all ingredients except ribs in a large mixing bowl and allow marinade to sit for 15 to 30 minutes, letting flavors blend. Arrange ribs on a large roasting pan in a single layer. Pour marinade over the ribs, covering completely. Rub the marinade into the ribs. Position roasting rack about 3" above the coals. Remove ribs from the marinade and save marinade in a separate bowl. Place ribs directly on the grill and sear 10 minutes on one side. Remove ribs, raise rack another 2," and cover with foil. With a fork, poke several holes in the foil for ventilation. Place ribs on the foil and cover with remaining marinade. Cook and turn the ribs every 5 minutes, basting often for about 40 minutes, until crusty and brown on the outside. Serves 4.

Take time out for a picnic!
Make a quick and easy salad with
bow-tie pasta, flaked salmon,
green onions and blanched peas.
Toss with low-cal Italian dressing.
Serve crusty French bread, melon,
prosciutto, and a dry white wine
(or chilled, sparkling water)
alongside and let the world go by.

Steamers

A bucket of steamers served with ice-cold beer is an East Coast tradition. Here's an easy microwave version in a delicious light sauce.

2 dozen soft-shell clams, well-scrubbed
1 T. salt
1 T. cornmeal
½ c. dry white wine
½ c. water
4 T. sweet butter
2 shallots, peeled and chopped
2 T. fresh parsley, chopped
2 cloves garlic, minced
ripe red tomato, diced

Cover clams with cold water in a large bowl. Sprinkle with salt and cornmeal. Let stand for about 1 hour. Rinse and drain. Put all other ingredients in a large microwave-safe casserole dish and stir. Microwave on high, uncovered, 5 minutes. Add clams, cover, and microwave 5 or 6 minutes, or until clams open. Serves 4.

Grilled Jumbo Shrimp

Alternate the shrimp with ripe cherry tomatoes on the skewer.

¼ c. soy sauce
1 c. orange juice
¼ c. olive oil
4 T. sugar
3 garlic cloves, minced
1 T. fresh ginger, finely chopped
1 T. lemon zest
2 lbs. jumbo shrimp, peeled and deveined
cherry tomatoes

In a small bowl, whisk together marinade ingredients. Add shrimp and marinate in refrigerator for at least 1 hour, stirring occasionally. Thread shrimp and cherry tomatoes onto skewers and barbecue about 2 minutes on each side, basting occasionally with marinade. Serves 6.

Create an edible centerpiece for your garden party...cut floral shapes from your favorite rolled sugar cookie recipe. Add a long skewer-type stick and bake as directed. Decorate the cookies as desired and poke them into a prepared flowerpot. Your guests can then pick a "flower" for dessert.

Teriyaki Steak Strips

Leave in marinade overnight for extra-flavorful steak.

¾ c. teriyaki sauce
1 T. fresh ginger, finely chopped
2 T. dry sherry
1 large beef top cut round steak, trimmed well and cut into strips

In small bowl, combine teriyaki sauce, ginger and sherry. Marinate the steak strips in refrigerator for 6 to 8 hours, turning occasionally. Remove steak from marinade; discard marinade. Put steak cubes on skewers and grill for about a half an hour or until desired doneness.

Anchor the four corners of your picnic tablecloth with bricks. You can paint the bricks to match the occasion, using them over and over again. For a birthday party, tie ribbons of helium balloons through the holes in the bricks. Instant celebration!

Rose Petal Sandwiches

8 oz. pkg. cream cheese, softened
3 T. rose water
12 thin slices white bread, crusts removed
6 unsprayed roses, red or pink

Mix cream cheese and rose water into a smooth spread; divide evenly among slices of bread, spreading very carefully on all pieces to edge. Cover each bread slice with rose petals, pressing them well into cheese spread. Cover and firm in refrigerator. After firming, cut in half, then fourths. Place on plate garnished with several roses. Other edible flowers may be used in sandwiches or for garnishes on plates, or cakes, or floated in beverages...try nasturtiums, Johnny jump-ups, marigolds, or violets.

Light Fare

Raspberry French Toast

¾ c. fat-free egg substitute
½ t. vanilla
½ t. ground cinnamon
½ c. 1% milk or skim milk
nonstick spray
8 slices "Texas toast" bread or
    French bread, sliced
2 c. raspberries*
¼ c. low-cal maple
    syrup

In a medium bowl, beat egg substitute, vanilla, cinnamon, and milk. Dip bread on both sides. Fry on griddle with no-stick spray, using medium heat until brown. Top with berries and syrup.

*blackberries may be substituted for raspberries.

Apricot Waffles

This is good served with an assortment of fresh fruit.

12 frozen waffles (or make your own)
6 T. light apricot preserves
8 oz. container nonfat vanilla yogurt
2 t. honey
2 c. strawberries, sliced

Heat waffles according to package. Spread 6 waffles with 1 tablespoon preserves; top each with a plain waffle. In a small bowl, combine yogurt and honey and blend well. To serve: Place 1 waffle sandwich on each plate, top with yogurt mixture and strawberries. Serve at once. Makes 6 servings.

Country Breakfast Casserole

This is light, only 5 grams of fat per serving!

1 T. vegetable oil
4 small potatoes, diced
1 sweet red pepper, diced
1 green pepper, diced
1 small onion, minced
1½ c. egg substitute
1 c. skim milk
2 T. flour
¼ t. black pepper
4 oz. low-fat
    Cheddar cheese, shredded
8 oz. pkg. meatless breakfast link sausage,
    chopped
vegetable cooking spray

Heat oil in medium skillet. Fry potatoes in oil until golden. Add peppers and onion. Mix egg substitute, milk, flour, black pepper, cheese, and breakfast links in mixing bowl. Fold in hot potato mixture. Coat a 12" × 8" baking dish with vegetable cooking spray. Pour potato mixture into baking dish. Bake at 350° for 45 minutes. Makes 8 servings.

Note: A small bag of frozen seasoned hash brown potatoes can be used instead of potatoes, onion, and sweet peppers.

Low-Fat Chicken Italiano

4 boneless, skinless chicken breasts
1 bottle low-fat or nonfat Italian salad dressing
2 c. bread crumbs
1 clove garlic, finely minced
1 T. Parmesan cheese
2 T. Italian herbs mixture (oregano, basil, marjoram, thyme, savory, rosemary and sage)
1 T. parsley flakes
no-stick spray

Marinate chicken breasts overnight in the Italian salad dressing in the refrigerator. Mix remaining dry ingredients. Shake excess off chicken breasts and then roll in bread crumb and seasonings mix. Spray baking sheet lightly with no-stick spray. Bake uncovered in 325° oven for approximately 45 minutes. Serves 4.

HEALTHY RECIPE SUBSTITUTIONS

Instead of: 1 c. butter or solid shortening
Use: 1 c. margarine or ¾ c. vegetable oil

Instead of: 1 c. sour cream
Use: 1 c. low-fat plain yogurt,
1 cup low-fat cottage cheese, blended
or 1 c. low-fat ricotta cheese

Instead of: 1 egg, whole
Use: ¼ c. egg substitute, 2 egg whites
or 1 egg white plus 1 t. vegetable oil

Instead of: 2 whole eggs
Use: 2 egg whites plus one whole egg

Instead of: 1 oz. baking chocolate
Use: 3 T. cocoa plus 1 T. vegetable oil

Multi-Vegetable Pasta

¼ c. light olive oil
1 medium onion, chopped
1 clove garlic, minced
½ c. fresh parsley, chopped
5 c. raw vegetables, chopped into ¾" pieces*
1 c. tomato sauce
¼ t. black pepper
½ t. dried basil leaves
½ t. dried oregano leaves
12 oz. tubular cooked
    pasta, like rigatoni
    or ziti
2 T. olive oil (optional)
Parmesan cheese, grated

Heat olive oil in a heavy saucepan over medium heat. Add onion, garlic, and parsley. Cook and stir for 2 minutes. Add denser vegetables first and cook over medium-high heat, stirring constantly for 3 to 4 minutes. Add remaining vegetables and tomato sauce and cook, stirring for 3 to 4 more minutes. Add pepper, basil, and oregano. Toss with cooked pasta, olive oil, and Parmesan cheese.

*Tasty vegetable combinations:
• onions, cauliflower, peas, carrots, zucchini, green pepper
• carrots, zucchini, radishes, asparagus, cucumber, onion
• peas, red pepper, carrots, celery, green onions
• broccoli, cauliflower, carrots, frozen peas, olives
• red and green peppers, corn, tomatoes, celery
• asparagus, carrots, celery, mushrooms

Other easy add-ins:
• julienne turkey breast (thin strips)
• chopped cooked chicken
• flaked canned salmon or tuna
• Swiss cheese

Catch of the Day in Foil

Get creative with this recipe! Use celery, tomatoes...any combination of veggies that go well with fish. This is also one of those wonderful opportunities to experiment with herbs. Add small amounts of marjoram, basil, or garlic.

2 haddock, flounder, sole, or any white fish
    fillets (approx. 4 to 5-ozs. each)
2 small green onions, finely chopped
2 t. fresh chives, minced
4 t. lemon juice
¼ t. paprika
1 c. peeled carrots, thinly sliced
4 mushrooms, thinly sliced
1 c. zucchini, thinly sliced
½ t. dill weed
pepper to taste

Preheat oven to 450°. Cut two sheets of aluminum foil large enough to enclose each fillet. Place a fillet in the center of each sheet, top each with half of the above ingredients. Fold the foil over each fillet, sealing edges very tightly. Place each package on a cookie sheet and bake for 15 to 20 minutes, or until fish flakes easily and veggies are tender to the fork. Serve guests fillets wrapped in their own silver pouches. Be careful as you unfold the foil, so you are not burned by the escaping steam. Serves 2.

Can't grill outside due to weather? Use your oven broiler, waiting until the last few minutes of cooking to baste meat and veggies.

Vegetable Casserole

Great flavor! My husband's favorite summer dish! Add corn on the cob and you have a meal.

3 onions, sliced
3 T. olive oil
4 medium potatoes, thinly sliced
2 medium zucchinis, thickly sliced
1 small eggplant, sliced thin
salt and pepper to taste
2 green peppers, sliced
1 T. olive oil
1 t. basil
½ t. garlic, minced
3 large tomatoes,
    peeled and sliced

In a heavy casserole pan, sauté two of the onions in the oil until tender. Add the potatoes and cook until lightly browned. Add the zucchini and eggplant in two layers. Season with salt and pepper. Make a layer of the remaining onion slices and green pepper. Drizzle the tablespoon of olive oil over all and sprinkle with basil and garlic. Top with tomatoes and season again. Cover, bring to a boil, and simmer gently about 25 minutes or until vegetables are tender. Serve hot, spooning down to the bottom to catch all layers. Serves 6.

For a light and summery meal, serve poached fish—either hot or cold! Simply place your favorite fish in a simmering pan, and cover with fresh herbs, sliced onion, salt, and a few bay leaves. Cover with a little white wine (optional) and water. Simmer uncovered until the fish flakes easily. Serve with a cold rice salad and sliced tomatoes for a wonderful and light meal.

Everyone is trying to eat a little lighter, especially in the summer. Substitute applesauce for vegetable oil in your favorite recipes. This will cut back on the fat, and it tastes great!

Tarragon Chicken

I make this all the time. You can serve this wonderful dish over rice or mashed potatoes (my husband's favorite).

2 T. flour
salt and pepper to taste
2 or 3 chicken breast halves
2 t. olive oil
¼ c. brandy
¾ c. fresh tomato pulp, or tomatoes, finely diced
1 to 2 T. shallots, or onions, diced
¼ c. fat-free liquid dairy creamer
½ c. canned chicken broth
½ t. tarragon (I use dried)

Place flour, along with salt and pepper, in a paper bag. Add chicken breasts to bag, close top, and shake to coat. Sauté in olive oil (you may need a little nonstick cooking spray). When almost done, add brandy and light with a match; stand back (don't get burned). Remove chicken from pan. Put tomatoes through a food processor. Cook shallots in the same pan that you cooked chicken in; add the rest of the ingredients and cook on fairly high heat for about a minute. Return chicken to pan. Makes 2 or 3 servings.

Note: For reduced fat, remove skin from chicken before cooking.

Garden Chicken Casserole

This casserole is wonderful for garden teas, picnics, gatherings of family and friends or Sunday brunches. Make sure to have extra copies of this recipe for requests. It's a sure hit!

2 c. chicken broth
⅔ c. cooking sherry, divided
6 oz. pkg. long grain and wild rice mix
1 small onion, chopped
2 small carrots, grated
1 small green pepper, chopped
¼ c. butter or margarine
3 c. cooked chicken, diced
4 oz. can mushrooms, sliced
8 oz. pkg. cream cheese
2 c. (8 oz.) American cheese, shredded
1 c. evaporated milk
⅓ c. Parmesan cheese, grated
½ c. almonds

Garnish:
sliced carrot rounds and green onions

In a medium saucepan bring broth and ⅓ cup sherry to a boil. Add contents of rice package, cover and simmer over low heat 25 to 30 minutes or until all liquid is absorbed. In a dutch oven, sauté onion, carrots, and green pepper in butter until soft, about 5 minutes. Add rice, chicken, and mushrooms, mixing well. Place cream cheese, American cheese, and milk in a saucepan and melt over medium heat, stirring until smooth. Add to dutch oven with remaining sherry, mixing thoroughly. Pour into a buttered 13" x 9" x 2" casserole dish. Top with Parmesan cheese and almonds. Cover and bake in a preheated 350° oven for 35 minutes; uncover and bake 15 minutes longer or until bubbly. If desired, garnish with carrot rounds and green onions to make a floral design on top of the casserole.

Note: Casserole may be refrigerated overnight before baking. If refrigerated, increase baking time to 45 minutes covered and 15 minutes uncovered.

Zucchini & Tomato Quiche

Great for a light dinner accompanied by a lettuce salad, wheat rolls, and a glass of wine.

2 c. zucchini, sliced
½ c. onion, chopped
1 T. butter
1 T. flour
½ c. Swiss cheese, shredded
1 large tomato, peeled and chopped (drain excess)
9" baked pie shell
6 eggs (can use egg substitute)
1 c. half & half
½ t. crushed basil
½ t. salt
⅛ t. pepper

In large skillet, over medium heat, sauté zucchini and onion in butter until lightly browned, approximately 5 minutes. Sprinkle zucchini mixture with flour. Add cheese and tomato, pour into pie shell. Beat together eggs, half & half, basil, salt, and pepper until well blended. Pour over vegetable mix. Bake at 375° for 30 to 35 minutes. Let stand 5 minutes before serving.

California Quiche

Great for brunches, and even weddings and baby showers! Serve with a fresh green salad and muffins.

1 deep-dish pie shell
¾ lb. hot Italian sausage
3 eggs, slightly beaten
1¾ c. milk
2 c. (8 oz.) Monterey jack cheese, shredded
4 oz. can green chillies, chopped

Prebake unpricked pie crust on a preheated cookie sheet in 450° oven for 6 minutes. Reduce temperature to 325°. Remove casing on sausage, brown in skillet, breaking up meat with a fork. Drain well. In a bowl combine eggs, milk, sausage, cheese, and chilies. Turn into partially baked pastry shell. Bake in 325 degree oven on a preheated cookie sheet for 45 minutes or until knife inserted comes out clean. Let stand about 10 minutes before serving. Makes 6 servings.

Lemon Thyme Stuffed Chicken

6 chicken breasts, skinned and boned
½ c. cream cheese
2 t. chives, chopped
1 t. fresh lemon thyme leaves
⅓ c. flour
1 t. paprika
½ t. salt
½ t. pepper
2 eggs
½ c. dry bread crumbs
½ c. Parmesan cheese
2 t. water
fresh thyme leaves, for garnish

Preheat oven to 350°. With a mallet, pound chicken breasts between sheets of plastic wrap until ⅛" thick. Roll with a rolling pin to even thickness. Spread a generous tablespoon of cream cheese lengthwise down center of each piece. Sprinkle each breast with 2 teaspoons chopped chives and 1 teaspoon lemon thyme leaves. Roll up jelly-roll style starting at narrow end. Tuck the sides under to seal. Combine flour, paprika, salt, and pepper on a plate. In a small bowl beat eggs and water. On another plate combine bread crumbs and Parmesan cheese. Dip chicken rolls in flour mixture, then in beaten egg and then in bread crumb mixture. Arrange with seam side down in a single layer in a greased baking pan. Bake for 20 to 25 minutes until juices run clear. Garnish with fresh thyme leaves.

Brunch Baked Eggs

Accompanying the eggs could be a variety of quick and yeast breads, fresh fruit cups/bowl, and champagne splashed with tangerine liqueur. If you decide to forego the ham, substitute Canadian bacon or smoked turkey alongside the eggs.

6 c. (24 oz.) Monterey jack cheese, shredded
12 oz. fresh mushrooms, sliced
½ medium onion, chopped
¼ c. sweet red pepper, thinly sliced
¼ c. margarine or butter, melted
8 oz. cooked ham, cut into julienne strips
8 eggs, beaten
1¾ c. milk
½ c. all-purpose flour
2 T. fresh chives, snipped (basil, tarragon, thyme or oregano can also be used)
1 T. parsley, snipped

Sprinkle 3 cups cheese in the bottom of a 13" × 9" × 2" baking dish. In a saucepan, cook the mushrooms, onion, and red pepper in the margarine until vegetables are tender but not brown. Drain well. Place vegetables over the cheese. Arrange ham strips over vegetables. Sprinkle remaining 3 cups cheese over ham. Cover and chill in refrigerator overnight. To serve, combine eggs, milk, flour, chives, and parsley. Pour over cheese layer. Bake at 350° about 45 minutes. Let stand 10 minutes. Serve ham alongside eggs. Serves 12.

Why use floppy paper plates for your picnic when plastic plates make eating so much easier? Easy to clean, earth-friendly, and inexpensive.

Salmon with Dill Sauce

This salmon tastes best when served warm or at room temperature.

2 to 3 lb. salmon fillet
½ c. soy sauce
1 t. black pepper, freshly cracked
½ c. heavy cream
¼ c. water
¼ c. olive oil
½ c. brown mustard
4 t. sugar
½ c. fresh dill, chopped

To prepare salmon, rinse and pat dry. Place skin side down on foil-lined pan and rub with soy sauce. Season with pepper and broil for 12 to 15 minutes. To prepare dill sauce, whisk remaining ingredients together. To serve, pour sauce over individual servings of salmon.

Here's a foolproof method for grilling fish that'll keep it from falling apart and disappearing into the grill...make a "boat" out of a double thickness of aluminum foil. The boat will keep the fish moist and intact, yet still give it that unmistakable grilled flavor. Place the fish fillet (no more than 1" thick) in the center of the foil and fold over the edges, crimping to form a 1" edge all the way around the fish to catch drippings. Put seasonings over the fish and cook, boat and all, uncovered, on top of the grill for 8 to 10 minutes, or until fish flakes easily with a fork. There's no need to turn the fish. To serve, top with some of the juices in the boat.

Chicken Piquant with Pinot Noir Sauce

A festive choice for Easter or any special occasion.

4 chicken breasts
1 bottle Pinot Noir (dry red wine)
3 garlic cloves, peeled and sliced
2 T. sugar
½ c. plus 1 T. raspberry vinegar
1 T. olive oil
5 T. butter
¼ lb. fresh mushrooms, sliced
salt and freshly ground pepper
Garnish: fresh raspberries and grapes

Marinate chicken in 2 cups wine for at least 1 hour. Meanwhile, combine ½ cup wine, garlic, sugar, and 1 tablespoon raspberry vinegar in saucepan. Bring to boil over high heat, dissolving sugar. Reduce heat, cover and cook until garlic is tender, about 12 minutes. Uncover, increase heat to high. Cook until liquid is reduced to a thick syrup and the garlic is glazed, approximately 10 to 15 minutes. Stir in remaining raspberry vinegar. Heat oil and 1 tablespoon butter in skillet. Sauté chicken. Set aside. Sauté mushrooms in same skillet. Remove to a platter with chicken. Add sauce to skillet. Cook on high until syrupy. Stir in remaining 4 tablespoons butter, salt, and pepper. Return chicken and mushrooms to skillet. Toss gently until heated through. Arrange chicken on platter and pour sauce with mushrooms over the chicken. Garnish with red raspberries and grapes.

Poached Salmon

Serve on an elegant platter with dill sauce.

4 6-oz. pieces of fresh salmon, wrapped in parchment paper
Court Bouillon
Dill sauce

In a large saucepan, cover wrapped salmon with court bouillon. Cook in boiling water for about 8 minutes. Remove salmon from liquid and remove paper carefully.

Court Bouillon:
1 c. celery, chopped
1 c. onion, chopped
1 t. black peppercorns
2 T. fresh parsley, chopped
2 T. fresh tarragon, chopped
2 c. vermouth
½ lemon
1 t. salt

Combine all ingredients in a medium saucepan and bring to a boil. Reduce heat and simmer for 8 minutes.

Dill Sauce:
1 c. sour cream
1 c. mayonnaise
2 T. fresh dill, chopped
2 T. lemon juice
salt and pepper to taste

Combine all ingredients in a blender and blend until smooth.

Rotini with Feta, Tomatoes, and Olives

Serve with warm crusty bread.

¼ c. extra virgin olive oil
2 8-oz. cans crushed tomatoes
1 c. black olives, drained and sliced
1 c. feta cheese, crumbled
16 oz. rotini pasta, cooked

Heat olive oil in a large skillet. Stir in the tomatoes, olives, and cheese and heat through. Add pasta to tomato mixture and toss well. Makes 4 servings.

There are many imported olives you can try in pastas and salads... huge and meaty Alfonsos, sharp and spicy Sicilians, and flavorful Ligurias from Italy; rich Calamatas and Royals from Greece; tender, savory Nicoise and crisp Picholines from France...ask to try a variety of olives at your local gourmet deli.

Summer Vegetable Pizza

This is a lovely summer appetizer or lunch and can be made ahead of time. Fresh fruit, iced mint tea, and summer vegetable pizza served under a shady tree is a perfect way to curl up with a **Gooseberry Patch** book and dream!

Crust and sauce:
1 tube refrigerated crescent rolls
2 8-oz. pkgs. cream cheese
1 ½ T. mayonnaise or yogurt
1 t. dillweed

Press crescent rolls onto a 13" pizza pan or baking stone, pinching seams together to seal. Bake at 350° until lightly browned. Let crust cool completely. Soften cream cheese and mix together with mayonnaise and dillweed. Spread evenly over top of the cooled crust.

Topping:
(All finely chopped) zucchini, mushrooms, green peppers, green onions, tomatoes, cucumbers (well drained), grated carrots. Thinly slice some to use as a garnish. Sprinkle a layer of each vegetable over cheese layer. Chill before serving. Cut in wedges or squares. Makes one pizza.

Broiled Chicken Breasts with Lime

Serve with a garnish of avocado and lime slices.

2 T. honey
3 T. lime juice
2 T. lime zest, grated
½ t. cumin
⅓ c. tequila
4 skinless, boneless chicken breasts
avocado slices and lime slices, for garnish

Preheat broiler and position rack about 4" below broiler. In medium bowl, whisk together honey, lime juice, lime zest, cumin, and tequila. Dredge chicken breast through marinade to coat thoroughly. Broil for 6 to 8 minutes, turning once and basting several times.

APPETIZING IDEAS

• Serve peeled and sliced kiwi fruit and melon on a platter along with thin slices of rolled-up prosciutto.

• Hollow out a watermelon and fill with honeydew, cantaloupe, and melon balls, along with strawberries and grapes.

• Mix softened cream cheese with crushed, drained pineapple, chopped pecans, chopped green pepper, and salt-free seasoning. Serve with crackers.

• Unwrap a loaf of party rye bread and spread with mayonnaise. Top with chopped olives, tomato, sweet onion, bacon bits, and grated cheese. Broil until bubbly.

• Mix chopped artichoke hearts with grated Parmesan cheese and mayonnaise. Add a bit of chili powder. Spread on mini-bagels and broil until lightly browned.

• Wrap thin slices of baked ham and Muenster cheese around artichoke hearts, place on top of bread rounds, and broil until cheese begins to melt.

• Unwrap an 8 oz. block of cream cheese and pour salsa over the top. Serve with crackers.

GARNISHES

Garnishes are great, because they add fun to your food and make any plate look even more appetizing. It's easy to add some simple elegance to your meal with a few little touches. Here are some ways to make magic with garnishes:

Colorful Citrus Wheels
Slice an orange, a lemon, and a lime into ¼-inch rounds. Cut halfway through each round, to the center. Using two hands, hold each side of the cut slice and twist them in opposite directions so the ends serve as a base, and the top half of the round will stand upright. Place on salad plates, or decorate the rim of a salmon platter. Have fun arranging the colors!

Radish Roses
Clean radishes thoroughly. Trim the top and bottom off the radish so that it's flat on both ends. Cut an X into the top of the radish, making a slice about ¾ of the way down. Turn the radish and make another X so that you have 8 equal cut portions. Soak covered with ice water for about 20 minutes, and the "roses" will open.

Scallion Starbursts
Trim off bulb and top of scallion. Using a sharp paring knife, make several 1- or 2-inch-long cuts on each end of the scallion, leaving about 2 inches in the middle. Soak for 15 minutes in ice water. The strands will curl open.

Country Quiche

A clever quiche that forms its own crust while baking.

3 eggs
½ c. biscuit mix
½ c. butter, melted
1½ c. milk
¼ t. salt
dash of pepper, freshly ground
1 c. Swiss cheese, shredded
½ c. smoked ham, cooked and cubed

Preheat oven to 350°. Grease a 9" pie pan. Place all ingredients except cheese and ham in blender, and blend well. Pour mixture in pan. Sprinkle cheese and ham on top. Press gently below surface with back of spoon. Bake for 45 minutes. Let stand 10 minutes before cutting.

Side Dishes

Stuffed Zucchini

Zucchinis are so plentiful in the summertime and new recipes are always welcome...especially tasty ones like this.

½ c. bread crumbs
2 T. Parmesan cheese
4 T. butter, softened
1 clove garlic, minced
½ c. onion, chopped
1 large tomato, peeled, seeded and chopped
2 medium zucchini, seeded, pulp set aside
salt and pepper to taste

Preheat oven to 350°. In a small dish, toss bread crumbs, cheese, and 2 tablespoons butter; set aside. In remaining butter, sauté garlic and onion until soft. Add tomatoes and zucchini pulp; heat through and mix well. Place zucchini shells in greased baking dish and fill with stuffing. Top with bread crumb mixture. Cover and bake for 30 minutes. Season to taste with salt and pepper and serve right away.

Bootlegger Beans

I tried this as the title intrigued me. Now I make three batches at a time...love it!

3 strips bacon
1 small onion, chopped
15 oz. can pork and beans
1 T. brown sugar
2 T. vinegar
2 T. catsup

Dice strips of bacon and fry. When partially fried, add onion. When onion is slightly browned, pour off most of grease and add pork and beans, sugar, vinegar, and catsup. Stir well and cover. Serves 4.

Fresh Asparagus with Tomato Vinaigrette

Just hold the asparagus by both ends and snap off the woody stems…they'll naturally break right where they should!

½ t. salt
1 lb. fresh asparagus
3 T. virgin olive oil
1½ T. white wine vinegar
½ t. honey
2 large tomatoes, seeded and chopped

Cover bottom of medium saucepan with about 1 inch of water and bring to rolling boil. Add salt and asparagus and boil for about 3 to 5 minutes, until tender. Drain. In another saucepan, heat olive oil and stir in vinegar and honey. Add tomatoes and heat through. To serve, pour tomato vinaigrette over asparagus.

> For a real treat, let the kids pitch a tent in the back yard and sleep under the stars.

> Have a "white elephant swap" at your family reunion. Ask everyone to bring something they'd like to get rid of…the more humorous the better. Have everyone take a number. Display all the "white elephants" on a table. At the end of the day, the person with #1 gets to choose his or her favorite item. The person with #2 has her choice, and so on until the "family heirlooms" are all gone.

Summer Squash Casserole

This was always a favorite summertime casserole. Squash is not always a favorite with children, but they love this casserole.

2 lb. (6 c.) yellow summer squash, sliced
¼ c. onion, chopped
1 can cream of chicken or cream of celery soup
1 c. sour cream
1 c. carrots, shredded
8 oz. pkg. herb stuffing mix
½ c. margarine, melted

Cook squash and onion in boiling salted water for 5 minutes. Drain. Mix soup and sour cream. Stir in shredded carrots. Add squash and onion. Combine stuffing and margarine. Spread half of stuffing mixture in a 9" square pan. Spoon on vegetable mixture. Sprinkle with remaining stuffing. Bake at 350° for 30 minutes. Be sure it is heated through.

Easy Red Potato Frittata

Mom will love this for breakfast with a toasted English muffin and fresh berries on the side.

3 egg whites
1 egg
2 T. chives, chopped
⅛ t. salt
⅛ t. pepper, freshly ground
nonstick cooking spray
½ c. baby red potatoes, diced
¼ c. red pepper, chopped
½ broccoli flowerets
⅓ c. water
½ t. vegetable oil
fresh chives

In mixing bowl, beat together egg whites, egg, one tablespoon chives, salt, and pepper. Lightly coat bottom of skillet with nonstick spray. Sauté potatoes until golden. Add pepper, broccoli and water, and cook covered about 3 minutes, until potatoes are tender. Uncover and cook until liquid has cooked away. Add oil to vegetables and toss until well coated. Add egg mixture. Cook until eggs begin to set, then stir well. Cover and continue cooking until eggs are set, but frittata is still moist on top. Remove cover and place under heated broiler until crisp and browned on top. Serve immediately, topped with fresh chives.

Tomato Frittata

Can be topped with various fresh vegetables… try black olives and mushrooms.

3 T. olive oil
4 eggs, slightly beaten
3 cherry tomatoes, thinly sliced
1 large scallion, thinly sliced
5 fresh sage leaves

Heat olive oil in heavy skillet. Pour in eggs and cook over medium heat for 4 to 6 minutes, drawing eggs away from sides and letting uncooked eggs run to the sides to cook. Add tomatoes, scallions, and sage and heat through for another minute or two.

Roasted Corn with Rosemary Butter

What could be better than fresh, sweet corn, roasted in the husk?

6 ears fresh corn, in husk
¼ c. butter, softened
1 t. fresh rosemary leaves, chopped

Pull back husks on corn, leaving them attached. Rinse corn and remove silk. Pat corn dry. In small bowl, mix together butter and rosemary; brush all over corn. Replace husks and roast corn on top of the grill for about 15 minutes, turning every so often until tender.

Sage ☆ Dill ☆ Mint ☆ Parsley ☆ Thyme

Quick, refreshing cooler...steep 8
mint tea bags in 2 cups of boiling water.
Add 2 cups of orange juice, 1½ cups lemonade,
2 cups crushed ice, and 2 cans of ginger ale.
Garnish with orange slices.

Sautéed Tomatoes with Tarragon

Garnish with fresh tarragon.

1 T. butter
1 T. olive oil
2 large, ripe tomatoes, sliced ½" thick
1 T. fresh tarragon, chopped
freshly ground black pepper to taste
dash of cayenne pepper
fresh tarragon for garnish

Heat the butter and oil in a large iron skillet over medium heat. Add tomato slices and sprinkle with the spices. After 2 or 3 minutes the tomatoes should be brown. Flip them over and cook through.

Many vegetables can be freshened by soaking in cold water. To crisp celery, carrots, or lettuce, wrap in a damp towel or place in a plastic bag and refrigerate for an hour.

Crab~Potato Cakes

Garnish these cakes with fresh, red tomato slices, and basil leaves.

2 T. mayonnaise
⅛ t. hot pepper sauce
2 egg whites, lightly beaten
¼ t. dry mustard
¾ t. lemon zest, grated
1½ t. fresh lemon juice
⅛ t. salt
2 t. celery, finely chopped
3 T. parsley, minced
1 T. green onions, finely chopped
2 red potatoes, boiled and shredded
½ lb. fresh crabmeat
½ c. dry bread crumbs
2 t. vegetable oil
tomato slices and bay leaves,
    for garnish

In a medium bowl, combine mayonnaise, hot pepper sauce, egg whites, mustard, lemon zest, lemon juice, and salt. Add celery, parsley, onions, potatoes, and crabmeat; stir well. Make 6 cakes out of mixture and dredge through bread crumbs. In non-stick skillet, heat one teaspoon oil over medium heat. Cook 3 cakes at a time, adding remaining oil to skillet after first batch. Makes 6 crab cakes.

Spicy Grilled Vegetables

Place directly on the grill for true smoky flavor.

3 large carrots, sliced lengthwise
4 medium potatoes, sliced diagonally
1 T. lime juice
⅓ c. olive oil
2 T. onion, chopped
½ t. salt
¼ t. pepper, freshly ground
½ t. cumin
2 large zucchini, sliced crosswise

Place carrots and potatoes in medium saucepan and cover with water. Over high heat, boil for 10 minutes. Drain and set aside. In another bowl, combine lime juice, olive oil, onion, salt, pepper, and cumin. Add potato mixture and zucchini slices tossing to coat well. Let stand for about 15 minutes allowing flavors to blend. Grill vegetables, turning once (about 3 minutes on each side). Serve hot.

> A general rule of thumb for cooking vegetables covered or uncovered is that vegetables that grow underground should be cooked covered; while those that grow above-ground should be cooked uncovered. Cook vegetables with a minimum amount of water.

Rice Pilaf with Carrots

Delicious, low-fat, and perfect with chicken dishes!

1 T. vegetable oil
2 c. basmati rice, uncooked
¼ c. onion, chopped
2 cloves garlic, minced
4 c. chicken broth
½ t. salt
1 c. fresh carrots, finely chopped
½ c. green onions, chopped
3 T. pine nuts, toasted

Heat oil in a medium saucepan over medium-high heat. Add rice and onion; sauté 2 minutes. Add garlic; sauté 1 minute. Add broth and salt; bring to a boil. Cover, reduce heat, and simmer 7 minutes. Stir in carrots; cover and cook and additional 7 minutes or until liquid is absorbed. Remove from heat; stir in remaining ingredients. Let stand covered for 5 minutes, then fluff with a fork. Serves 7.

Desserts

Yogurt Smoothie

You'll need a blender for this recipe. It makes a nutritious, low-fat snack. Delicious and very filling.

1 small carton low-fat yogurt with fruit on bottom
1 banana (any combination of berries, peaches, strawberries, or any soft fruit can be included or substituted)*
½ c. fruit juice (orange, pineapple, etc.)
3 ice cubes

Put ingredients in blender and blend until smooth.

*You can use overripened fruit that you might otherwise be tempted to throw away.

Fudge–Topped Cherry Hearts

Prepared ingredients make these quick and easy to prepare!

8 oz. pkg. frozen puff pastry sheets, thawed
¾ c. cherry pie filling
8 t. fudge sauce (ice cream topping)
2 T. almonds, chopped

Preheat oven to 375°. Unfold pastry onto lightly floured surface. Using a heart-shaped cookie cutter, cut pastry into 8 hearts. Place hearts onto ungreased cookie sheet and bake for 15 to 18 minutes until golden. Cool and split hearts horizontally. Spoon cherry pie filling inside each heart and replace tops. To serve, heat fudge sauce until smooth and drizzle over hearts. Sprinkle with almonds and serve immediately. Serves 8.

Rose Geranium Cake

There are two preparations that must be done the night before making this cake and frosting…wrapping sticks of butter with leaves and making the rose geranium sugar for the frosting.

Prepare the night before:
For the cake:
24 rose geranium leaves
1 c. butter or margarine (use sticks)

Rinse leaves and wrap 5 or 6 leaves around each stick of butter. Wrap butter in foil or plastic wrap, refrigerate overnight.

Rose Geranium Sugar:
1½ c. sugar, divided
3 or 4 fresh rose geranium leaves

Pour ¾ cup sugar into a container with a tightly fitted lid. Wash rose geranium leaves, add to sugar container. Cover with another ¾ cup sugar. Cover container and let stand overnight.

Next day:
For the cake:
1¾ c. sugar
6 egg whites
3 c. cake flour, sifted
4 t. baking powder
½ t. salt
¾ c. milk
½ c. water
1 t. vanilla
butter

Remove leaves from butter (save for further use); gradually add sugar, creaming until light and fluffy. Add egg whites two at a time, beating well after each addition. Sift together flour, baking powder and salt. Combine milk, water, and vanilla. Alternately add dry ingredients and milk mixture to creamed mixture, beginning and ending with dry ingredients; beat smooth after each new addition. Grease and flour two 9" round or 8" round layer cake pans. Arrange 10 to 12 rose geranium leaves (including those saved from the butter) on bottom of each pan. Spoon batter over leaves and bake in 350° oven for 30 to 35 minutes or until done. Cool in pans for 10 minutes. Remove layers from pans and let cool on racks. Gently remove rose geranium leaves from bottom and discard.

For the frosting:
1½ c. rose geranium sugar
2 egg whites
⅓ c. cold water
¼ t. cream of tartar
dash of salt

Remove leaves from sugar. Place rose geranium sugar, egg whites, water, cream of tartar, and salt in top of double boiler (do not overheat). Beat one minute with electric beater. Place over, but not touching, boiling water. Cook, beating constantly until frosting forms stiff peaks (about 7 minutes). Remove from boiling water, beat until spreading consistency (about 2 minutes). Frost between layers and spread frosting to cover sides and top of 2-layer cake. Garnish frosted cake with candied rose geranium leaves made by rolling dampened leaves in sugar.

Hint: If the above recipe is too time-consuming, but you want a special cake…just cover the bottom of a cake pan with rose geranium leaves and pour batter for a pound cake, or even a plain white cake, over leaves. Bake and remove leaves from bottom after baking. Imparts a wonderful flavor to cake!

Picnic Chocolate Cake

2 c. flour
2 c. sugar
½ t. salt
2 sticks margarine
4 T. cocoa
1 c. water
2 eggs
1 t. soda
1 t. vanilla
½ c. buttermilk

In a large bowl mix together flour, sugar, and salt. In a small saucepan heat margarine, cocoa, and water. Stir chocolate mixture into flour mixture until smooth. Add eggs, soda, vanilla, and buttermilk. Mix until smooth and pour into a 13" × 9" pan. Bake at 375° for 15 to 20 minutes. Let cake stand for 5 minutes before frosting; frost while still warm.

Frosting:
1 lb. powdered
    sugar
1 stick margarine
4 T. cocoa
6 T. buttermilk

Put powdered sugar in a large bowl. In a saucepan melt (do not boil) margarine, cocoa, and buttermilk. Add to powdered sugar and mix well.

Blackberry Crumble

Top with freshly whipped cream.

1 lb. blackberries, rinsed
6 to 8 T. sugar
½ c. butter or margarine
1⅔ c. whole wheat flour
⅔ c. rolled oats
½ c. soft brown sugar

Preheat oven to 350°. Line bottom of pie pan with blackberries and sprinkle sugar over them. In a mixing bowl, cut butter into flour and blend with pastry blender until crumbly. Stir in the oats and brown sugar and mix well. Sprinkle on top of the berries. Bake for 40 to 45 minutes until the top is golden.

To make an Easter basket cake, decorate the top of a white layer cake with green-colored coconut. Arrange jelly beans on top; then insert both ends of a long chenille wire into the cake to form the basket "handle." Twine silk flower stems around the handle.

Nectarine and Raspberry Crisp

A yummy summertime treat!

2 large nectarines, halved and pitted
⅓ c. apricot preserves
1 t. vanilla
2 c. fresh raspberries
½ c. all-purpose flour
⅓ c. brown sugar, packed
½ t. ground cinnamon
¼ t. ground nutmeg
⅓ c. butter or margarine
1 c. granola
¼ c. toasted slivered almonds, chopped coarsely
vanilla ice cream

Cut nectarines into ½" slices. In an 8" × 8" × 2" baking pan or dish or an 8" × 1½" round baking dish, stir together nectarines, preserves, and vanilla. Carefully fold in berries. In a bowl, combine flour, sugar, cinnamon, and nutmeg. Cut in butter until mixture resembles coarse crumbs. Add granola and almonds. Toss with a fork until mixed. Sprinkle this mixture over the fruit in the baking pan. Bake at 375° for 25 to 30 minutes or until topping is golden. Serve warm or at room temperature with ice cream. Makes about 6 servings.

Make an ice cream "watermelon"... line a big bowl with softened pistachio ice cream (this will be the rind), and set aside in freezer. Fold chocolate chips (for the seeds) into softened strawberry ice cream. Pour the strawberry ice cream into the bowl over the pistachio layer. Place bowl in the freezer. To serve, just remove ice cream from bowl and slice into watermelon-shaped wedges.

Watermelon Sorbet

A great-tasting cool treat!

¾ c. water
1 c. sugar
2 to 4 c. watermelon pulp, chopped and seeded
⅓ c. lemon juice
a rose geranium leaf or 1 t. rose water

Boil water and sugar gently for 4 minutes; cool. Put puréed fruit into a stainless bowl along with cooled water mixture, lemon juice, and rose geranium or rose water. Cover and freeze 4 hours. Process with whisk, freeze until mushy, about an hour. Beat again and freeze until firm. Serve.

STRAWBERRY PRESERVES

Serve over vanilla ice cream, or swirl into whipped cream for a strawberry "fool."

4 qts. small, ripe strawberries
9 c. sugar
juice of 1 lemon

Hull strawberries and layer them with sugar in a glass bowl. Cover and let stand overnight. Pour strawberry-sugar mixture into a deep, nonaluminum saucepan. Add lemon juice and heat to a boil. Let simmer 5 minutes. Return strawberry mixture to bowl, cover, and let stand 24 hours. Return strawberry mixture to pan and bring to a rapid boil until the syrup has thickened, about 30 minutes. Cool slightly. If not using right away, pack into sterilized jars according to the manufacturer's directions and process 10 minutes in a boiling water bath. Or, pack into freezer containers and freeze up to several months. The preserves can be refrigerated several weeks, if you don't intend to freeze them.

Independence Day Shortcake

Since these are really just scones, you can serve leftovers with fresh jam and butter. They freeze well, too!

2 c. flour
1 T. baking powder
½ t. salt
2 T. granulated sugar
¾ c. butter
1 egg
½ c. plus 1 T. cream
2 T. butter, melted
¼ c. sugar
strawberries and
    blueberries, about ¾ c. per serving
whipped topping or sweetened whipped cream

Mix together flour, baking powder, salt, and sugar Cut in butter until fine crumbs. Mix egg and cream together. Blend into dry ingredients. Knead dough lightly on floured surface. Divide dough in half. Pat out each half to about ½" thick. Cut one-half with round biscuit cutter and place on greased cookie sheet. Cut other half with star cookie cutter and place on greased cookie sheet. Bake in preheated 400° oven for 8 to 10 minutes or until done. After 6 minutes, brush stars with melted butter and sprinkle with red-tinted sugar. Continue baking until done. Wash and dry fruit, slice strawberries. Toss with 2 tablespoons sugar for each cup of fruit and chill for an hour or more. Assemble as follows (for each serving)...round scone, heaping spoon of topping or cream, ¾ cup fruit, star scone, small dollop of topping or cream, then top with a tiny American flag or whole berry. Serves 6 to 8.

Lemon Crunch Cookies

Serve with blueberry-lemon mousse and minty iced tea.

1 c. flour
¼ t. cream of tartar
½ t. baking soda
¼ c. margarine, softened
¾ c. sugar
1 t. lemon juice
1 T. lemon zest
1 egg
¼ t. allspice
¼ t. salt
1 c. quick oats
vegetable cooking spray

Preheat oven to 350°. In bowl, mix flour, cream of tartar, and baking soda; set aside. Cream margarine and gradually add sugar. Beat at medium speed until well blended. Add lemon juice, lemon zest, egg, allspice, and salt; beat well. Gradually add flour mixture and mix until combined. Stir in oatmeal. Drop dough by teaspoonful onto cookie sheets, and bake for 12 minutes. Makes 3½ dozen.

Cheesecake Cookies

⅔ c. brown sugar, packed
1 c. walnuts, chopped
2 c. flour
⅔ c. margarine, melted
16 oz. cream cheese, softened
½ c. sugar
2 eggs
2 T. lemon juice
4 T. milk
2 t. vanilla

Preheat oven to 350°. Mix brown sugar, walnuts, flour, and margarine together, until light and crumbly. Remove 2 cups for topping. Press remainder in 13" × 9" pan. Bake crust for 12 to 15 minutes. While baking, beat cream cheese and sugar until smooth. Beat in eggs, lemon juice, milk, and vanilla. Pour into crust. Top with reserved crumbs, and bake for 25 minutes. Cool thoroughly, cover, and refrigerate.

Bake a batch of your favorite cookies...
chocolate chip, peanut butter, oatmeal,
sugar...and sandwich different
flavors of ice cream inside.

Peach Crisp

Serve warm with fresh whipped cream or hand-
cranked vanilla ice cream.

½ c. brown sugar
½ c. flour
½ c. butter, chilled
  and sliced
¼ c. quick oats
8 fresh ripe peaches,
  peeled, pitted,
  and sliced
3 T. lemon juice
¼ t. nutmeg
¼ t. cinnamon

Preheat oven to 375°. In
a small mixing bowl, com-
bine brown sugar and flour.
Add butter and mix with
pastry blender until crumbly;
stir in oats. In a glass pie dish, toss
peaches with lemon juice, nutmeg, and
cinnamon. Sprinkle peaches liberally
with topping and bake for about 25
minutes. Makes 4 servings.

Ginger Coconut Tart

Buy the shredded coconut already prepared. You
may substitute fresh, ripe sliced pears if papayas
aren't available. Delicious!

1 prepared pie crust, baked
8 oz. cream cheese, room temperature
6 T. cream of coconut (canned)
3 T. sugar
1 c. sweetened shredded coconut, toasted
¼ c. crystallized ginger, chopped
2 large papayas, peeled and thinly sliced
½ c. apricot preserves

Bake pie crust according to package
directions (or make your own
favorite pie crust and bake until
golden brown). Beat cream cheese
with a mixer until smooth, then add
cream of coconut, sugar, ¾ cup of
the toasted coconut, and the ginger.
Spread filling in pie crust. Place
papaya slices in attractive arrangement on top of filling. In a small
saucepan, heat preserves over low
heat, stirring until melted. Brush preserves over the top of the tart. Sprinkle
remaining coconut over the top.
Refrigerate at least 1 hour, or until firm.

Never underestimate the power of a
popsicle to cool, refresh, and make you
feel like a kid again. Orange is the
hands-down best flavor.

136

Fresh Peach Ice Cream

This low-fat, creamy recipe tastes very rich…brings back memories of summer on the farm. Garnish with fresh mint.

5 c. 1% milk, divided
4 egg yolks
8 ripe peaches, peeled and mashed
2 T. freshly squeezed lemon juice
2½ T. pure vanilla extract
½ t. ground ginger
½ t. almond extract
2 14-oz. cans sweetened condensed skim milk

Combine 2½ cups of the milk and the egg yolks in a heavy saucepan and whisk well. Cook and stir over medium heat about 10 minutes, or until mixture will coat a spoon. (Do not overcook, or it will turn into scrambled eggs!) Combine egg mixture with remaining milk, peaches, and all remaining ingredients in a large bowl and stir well. Cover and chill. Pour mixture into the freezer section of an ice cream freezer. Freeze according to manufacturer's directions. Spoon into a container with a tight-fitting lid and freeze for an hour, or until completely firm. Serves 12 to 24, depending on portion size.

I scream, you scream,
we all scream for ice cream!
—Children's rhyme

TANTALIZING TOPPINGS

Hot Fudge

½ c. unsweetened cocoa powder
1 c. sour cream
1½ c. sugar
½ t. vanilla extract

In a double boiler, combine all ingredients, stirring until well mixed throughout. Cook over boiling water for about an hour, stirring until thick and creamy. Keep warm in a crockpot set to low heat.

Blueberry Syrup

1 c. blueberries
½ c. sugar
¼ vanilla bean, split lengthwise
¾ c. water
2½ T. freshly squeezed lemon juice

Combine blueberries, sugar, and vanilla bean in a medium saucepan. Add water and bring to a boil over medium-high heat. Reduce heat to low and simmer about 5 minutes. Remove vanilla bean and pour mixture into a blender. Add lemon juice and blend until smooth.

Easy Strawberry Ice Cream

Garnish with a ripe red strawberry and a wafer cookie. Vary the recipe with different fruits throughout the summer.

⅔ c. very cold buttermilk
1 t. orange extract
2 10-oz. pkgs. frozen strawberries, slightly thawed
fresh strawberries and wafer cookies, for garnish

Place buttermilk and orange extract into blender or food processor. Cut slightly thawed fruit into chunks and add to blender. Whirl until mixture is smooth and ice cream consistency. Serve immediately.

QUICK TOPPING IDEAS

Crushed chocolate sandwich cookies
Peanuts, cashews, or macadamia nuts
Colored sugar sprinkles
Chocolate jimmies
Crushed hard candies
Sweetened cocoa powder
(fill a big shaker full)
Chocolate chips and chunks
Butterscotch chips
Whipped topping, colored with a few
drops of food coloring just for fun
Fresh blueberries, strawberries,
raspberries, or blackberries
Honey
Crushed pineapple
and don't forget the maraschino cherries!

Deluxe Ice Cream Sandwiches

These chewy, thin, oatmeal cookies make for delicious sandwiches.

1½ c. sweet butter
3 c. uncooked rolled oats (not instant)
1½ T. flour
1 t. salt
1¾ c. sugar
2 t. vanilla extract
2 eggs, lightly beaten
½ gallon natural vanilla ice cream
sprinkles

Melt butter in a large saucepan over low heat. Let cool and add oats, flour, salt, sugar, and vanilla. Stir well to combine, then add eggs and mix thoroughly. On a baking sheet that has been covered with parchment and buttered, spoon 1½ tablespoons of batter for each cookie, leaving about 3" between cookies. Flatten cookies into circles. Bake at 450° until golden brown, about 15 minutes. Let cool. Makes 2 dozen. Unwrap a square block of vanilla ice cream and slice into 1"-thick slices, cutting into squares big enough to slightly overlap edges of cookies. Sandwich ice cream between cookies. Dip edges of sandwiches into sprinkles. Wrap individually and freeze until ready to serve.

Orange-Filled Napoleons

Easy to make and elegant to serve!

8 oz. pkg. frozen puff pastry sheets, thawed
2 c. softened vanilla ice cream
1 naval orange, peeled and thinly sliced
powdered sugar

Preheat oven to 375°. Unfold pastry and cut into 8 rectangles. Place on ungreased cookie sheet and bake for 20 minutes or until pastries are puffed and golden. Cool on wire rack. To serve, split pastries lengthwise. Spoon ice cream on one half; top with orange slices and replace pastry top. Dust with powdered sugar and serve immediately.

Wild Blueberry Ice

We're using frozen blueberries for ease of preparation...you can use fresh blueberries that you've simmered and stirred in a small amount of water and allowed to cool.

¼ c. sugar
½ c. water
15 oz. pkg. frozen blueberries in heavy syrup, thawed and syrup drained (reserve syrup)

In small saucepan, cook sugar and water over low heat until sugar dissolves. Remove from heat; add syrup from blueberries and half of the berries. Chill thoroughly. Freeze mixture in an ice cream maker according to manufacturer's instructions. Serve right away, topped with remaining blueberries.

Berries, grapes, and melon make a beautiful fruit cup when served in wine glasses.

Metric Conversions
(Approximate)

LENGTH ★

inches (in)	multiply by 2.5 to find	centimeters (cm)
feet (ft)	multiply by 30 to find	centimeters (cm)
yards (yd)	multiply by 0.9 to find	meters (m)

MASS ★

ounces (oz)	multiply by 28 to find	grams (g)
pounds (lb)	multiply by 0.45 to find	kilograms (kg)

VOLUME ★

teaspoons (tsp)	multiply by 5 to find	milliters (mL)
tablespoons (Tbsp)	multiply by 15 to find	milliters (mL)
fluid ounces (fl oz)	multiply by 30 to find	milliters (mL)
cups (c)	multiply by 0.24 to find	liters (L)
pints (pt)	multiply by 0.47 to find	liters (L)
quarts (qt)	multiply by 0.95 to find	liters (L)
gallons (gal)	multiply by 3.8 to find	liters (L)

TEMPERATURE ★ ★ ★ ★ ★ ★ ★ ★ ★ ★ ★ ★ ★ ★ ★ ★ ★ ★ ★

F degrees	subtract 32 and multiply by $5/9$ to find C degrees

Index

How Did Gooseberry Patch Get Started?

★ ★ ★ ★ ★ ★ ★ ★ ★ ★ ★ ★ ★ ★ ★ ★ ★ ★

Our catalog business called **Gooseberry Patch** started back in 1984, when we were young mothers of preschool children. As neighbors in Delaware, Ohio, we both loved collecting antiques and country decorating (and chatting over the backyard fence!). Though neither of us had experience (Jo Ann was a first-grade schoolteacher and Vickie, a flight attendant and legal secretary), we decided to try our hands at the mail-order business. Since our kids were small, this was perfect...we could operate the business from our homes and keep an eye on the kids!

After about five years, our "little" business grew too big for our basements and kitchen tables. What started out as a 12-page catalog with 40 products has grown bigger every year, with over 400 products at last count! Our shelves are filled with Santas, trees, trimmings, gift baskets, angels, snowmen, cookie cutters, candles, birdhouses, and our very own collection of country cookbooks. In the spring of 1997 we moved into our own building in the country, designed just for **Gooseberry Patch**!

Vickie & Jo Ann

Would you like to receive "A Country Store in Your Mailbox^SM"? For a 2-year subscription to our **Gooseberry Patch** catalog, simply send $3.00 to:

Gooseberry Patch
149 Johnson Drive
P.O. Box 190, Dept. Book
Delaware, OH 43015